Thank you, Joy Yoon, for writing a wonderful book that is so desperately needed in this troubled world today! **Discovering Joy: Ten Years in North Korea** *pulls back the curtain and allows us to look into the reality of a country full of loveable people. With your rich cross-cultural and educational background and with more than a decade of first-hand experience, along with your husband and three children among the people in North Korea, you cut right through the negative stereotypes that dominate our US news media and politics. You help us to discover the beauty of the children and the admirable courage of their parents. What a treasure you have given us in this excellent book!*

DON MOSLEY
FOUNDER, HABITAT FOR HUMANITY

Joy Yoon's book **Discovering Joy: Ten Years in North Korea** *is a paradigm shattering read, which delves into many of the misunderstandings between North Korea and the international community. Writing from over eleven years' experience working in country, Joy shares from first-hand knowledge. Her insights into the hearts and minds of the people of North Korea bring humanity and warmth to a country most commonly viewed as cold and dark. A must read for anyone desiring a better understanding of North Korea.*

GABE SEGOINE
AUTHOR, SURFING NORTH KOREA
EXECUTIVE DIRECTOR, LOVING NORTH KOREA MINISTRIES

Joy Yoon and her gifted husband Dr. Stephen Yoon, are among a handful of Americans who know North Korea from the inside out. For more than a decade, Dr. and Mrs. Yoon and their family have lived and worked in the city of Pyongyang in the Democratic People's Republic of Korea ("DPRK"). Joy was born in Illinois but grew up as the daughter of American professors in South Korea. Her new book, **Discovering Joy: Ten Years in North Korea**, *is fascinating. Joy's story not only introduces the reader to the everyday life of North Koreans, but is also the story of a dedicated couple living out the life of Christ in a most inspiring way. Near the end of the book, as she describes what it may take for the outside world to bridge the gap with North Korea, I was struck with how applicable her wise counsel might be to anyone dealing with a strained relationship where there is misunderstanding or hostility.*

John C. Bowling
President, Olivet Nazarene University

A provocative and thought-changing book on the typical stereotypes given to North Korea and a must read for those interested in knowing more about the country.

Wade Longcrier
Global aid worker to North Korea
Associate Pastor for Global & Community Outreach,
First Baptist Church Carollton, TX

Based on almost a decade of living inside North Korea and shaped by her experience growing up in South Korea, Joy Yoon provides a rare up-close view of formative elements that shape every day North Korean experience, mindset, history, and culture.

Scott Snyder
Author, South Korea at the Crossroads
Senior Fellow for Korea Studies,
Council on Foreign Relations

From her own experiences in the DPRK and her knowledgeable understanding of Korean history, Joy Yoon has written a narrative of the North Korean people that is different, personal and hopeful. So much is being written about North Korea these days. Much of it is the same story written in many different variations, but a single story only gives the reader one brush stroke to define a people. Joy has given us a different and vibrant stroke of the brush. If we truly want to understand and engage with the DPRK, then we must listen to all of the narratives. This is her and her family's narrative of ten years living with the people of DPRK as Americans. These are true experiences of what is possible and therefore what might actually become the future reality.

Ben and Liz Torrey
The Three Seas Center
(preparing the next generation for a unified korea)
Taebaek, South Korea

Discovering Joy

Ten Years in North Korea

Joy Yoon

Discovering Joy: Ten Years in North Korea
Published by Joy Yoon.

Some names and identifying details have been changed to protect the privacy of individuals.

2nd Edition
ISBN 979-8-700377-3-00

www.joyinnorthkorea.com

To my loving family,
and to the entire Ignis Community:
forty-plus field workers, home staff,
board members, volunteers,
donors and supporters.

CONTENTS

FOREWORD

When I first heard about an American couple living with their children inside North Korea for 10 years—caring for children with autism and cerebral palsy, with the North Korean government's permission and support—I couldn't believe it was true. But then, in 2015, I met Joy and Stephen Yoon. In the years since, due to my own work with a Christian agency in Northeast Asia, I have spent time with the Yoon family in Pyongyang and Beijing and South Korea. And I have come to believe their journey with the North Korean people is one of the most important stories in our times, a glimpse of what it's like when we welcome reconciliation into our broken and divided world.

It is that way of peace for which our world desperately yearns, and which we find in Joy's story. There are three important gifts of this book to keep in mind.

First, Joy's story helps us avoid what Nigerian novelist Chimamanda Adichie called "the danger of a single story." One reason the Korean peninsula has for decades been one of the most dangerous situations in the world is because fear has dominated all sides—North Korea, South Korea, and the U.S. Fear begets policies of fear, such that Americans rarely travel into North Korea and the average South and North Korean cannot cross the border, meet, share a meal, or even see one another up close. One result, as Joy says, is that North Korea is one of the most misunderstood countries in the world. Yet Joy's stories in this book reveal the humanity of North Koreans she has come to know: the teacher who strapped a girl who could not walk onto her back, and carried her to class every day; the guide her children came to call "Uncle"; the North Korean teachers who tirelessly taught their children at Pyongyang Korean School for Foreigners; the colleague who made a passionate appeal to his superiors on their behalf for "an American woman and her family and their sacrifice and heart for North Korea"; the officials who saw the positive impact of their cerebral palsy work and gave permission to set up pediatric rehabilitation centers in all ten provincial hospitals. In helping us see multiple stories about North Korea, about people who care about other people, Joy gives us hope that when our "single story" is stretched, a new future is possible.

A second wonderful gift of Joy's book is the message that in any place of distrust, from families to countries, peace requires both acceptance of differences and willingness to change on the part of all parties. Joy helps us see how North Korea and South Korea have become two very different worlds which, while speaking the same language, do not even use the same names to refer to each other's countries. In showing us the challenges she has faced from all three sides—North Koreans, South Koreans, and Americans—Joy shows us how seeking peace means becoming a bridge between divided people. But bridges get walked on from both sides. Being a bridge between deep differences is costly. It is painful. For Joy, being a bridge and seeking to build heart-felt relationships required time and learning patience, kindness, gentleness, and self-control. In other words, building trust became a journey into deeper intimacy with Christ. The deep, heart-felt relationships Joy and her family developed with many North Korean people is an image of the hard, cross-border work that is required in any place of deep distrust. For those involved in this kind of work, that can become a journey into deeper holiness.

The third gift of Joy's book is to mirror the truth that reconciliation requires sacrifice. In Joy and her family's life, we see that seeking reconciliation is difficult and costly. There are days you don't know if you can take another step. Yet Joy's story is ultimately a story of light, not darkness. This calls us to see and follow the pathway of Jesus, who "for the joy set before him ... endured the cross" (Hebrews 12:2). Without joy the journey of seeking peace where there is distrust and division is not worth it.

Yet in the most unlikely place called North Korea, Joy discovered .... joy. In the end, the story of the Yoon family is not about heroism. It is about beauty. It is about the joy that most matters and is most meaningful in this world—the joy of relationship, of miracles given when we are at the end of our rope, of giving and receiving in ways that bind us together with the most unlikely people, of strangers becoming precious companions. It is the best kind of story of reconciliation.

Dr. Chris Rice
Representative for Northeast Asia,
Mennonite Central Committee
Senior Fellow for Northeast Asia,
Duke Divinity School

PREFACE

Understand North Korea? Really?

As you read this simple book, my hope is that you will come to know and understand North Korea a little better. And that perhaps, just perhaps, new understanding might lead us all to successful engagement with this nation and her people. As a humanitarian worker who lived in North Korea for eleven years, I feel that I gained a deeper level of understanding into the heart of North Koreans. Although we are both U.S. citizens, my husband and I grew up in South Korea and already had that native knowledge of Korean culture and language as a foundation. The better we came to know North Koreans, however, the more we realized that what we thought we knew of them had often missed the mark completely.

Recently again, North Korea has been at the center of world controversy. Their development of nuclear weapons has put the United States on edge as it has all of Korea's bordering countries and indeed the world. Is this country not at fault and to blame for pushing the world to the brink of war? This is no small matter that we can ignore.

North Korea is surrounded by major world powers such as China, Russia, and U.S.-supported South Korea and Japan. A nuclear crisis with North Korea could very likely cause a third world war.

The DPRK's continuing development of nuclear weapons is in direct violation of their commitment as a member of the United Nations. But despite warnings from the United States, the U.N., and most of the rest of the world, North Korea remains largely undeterred, on a steady course towards nuclear proliferation. Years of sanctions did not throw North Korea off its determined course. They in fact did not deviate from it until the North and the South began discussing a treaty to end the Korean War. Why is this?

There are only a handful of foreigners in North Korea. Most from the West who live in North Korea and are not diplomats or part of large international organizations such as the United Nations are there for benevolent reasons. Whether for humanitarian or business purposes, our intent has been to serve ordinary North Koreans. We believe that through engagement with people in the nation, barriers will begin to break down and trust will have room to grow.

At the beginning of September 2017, the U.S. Department of State issued a travel restriction for North Korea. Approximately 200 U.S. citizens living and working in North Korea were asked to leave the country. We were forced to leave our homes in North Korea and relocate to other parts of Asia or return to the United States. It was a sad day for us personally as well as a set-back to the projects we'd devoted years to diligently building.

It is only natural that the United States and South Korea should be concerned about potential nuclear warfare with North Korea. North Korea has now boasted of being able to reach major cities on the mainland of the U.S. with intercontinental ballistic missiles carrying nuclear warheads. This would certainly put any nation on alert. But we should not only be concerned with the fact that North Korea has developed nuclear weapons. We should be concerned with the deeper issues and their root causes that set North Korea on this collision course with the world.

My husband and I believe that North Korea is perhaps one of the most misunderstood nations of the world. Why? Because our prejudicial biases prevent us from seeing them as people like ourselves. We depersonalize them, view them as the enemy and maintain the sort of confrontational stance that usually only ends in violence.

The last thing the world needs now is another

war, especially a world war that might involve nuclear destruction. Even the United States admits that war with North Korea would have catastrophic consequences.[1]

Experts have estimated that if war broke out again on the Korean Peninsula, millions of people would die.[2] Many of these deaths would be innocent civilians, including women and children. Given this reality, war simply cannot be an option.

We must consider the best alternative, which is negotiation. However, history has shown that talks with North Korea have rarely been successful. For years, the six nations of North and South Korea, the United States, Russia, China, and Japan attempted to come to agreeable compromises for all parties involved to no avail. Eventually, the six-party talks were abandoned, and tensions between North and South Korea as well as North Korea and the United States steadily increased until the Winter Olympics this year in 2018.

Then on April 26th, the presidents of North and South Korea met in the Demilitarized Zone on the 38th parallel. For the first time since Korea was divided, a North Korean President stepped foot on South Korean soil. Talks of peace began, and North Korea committed to dismantling their nuclear weapons facilities. Progress seemed rapid.

A meeting for President Trump and Chairman Kim Jong-Un was set for June 12th in Singapore.

Then suddenly, North Korea started threatening postponement of their meeting with President Trump. What prompted this? Joint military exercises between South Korea and the United States threatened North Korea's sense of trust and safety. But North Korea stated that they understood the need for joint military exercises at the April 26th meeting. So what was the problem?

These joint exercises were not standard training operations. They were specifically designed to prepare for a pre-emptive strike on North Korea. These actions were viewed by North Korea as a threat to peace on the Korean Peninsula. Trust was broken, and the threat that war would bring world-wide destruction came back into the picture. But after a letter from President Trump, the two presidents made history as they met at the Summit in Singapore for the first time since North Korea became a nation. The initial meeting went well, but whether or not current negotiations will be successful remains to be seen. What is the solution, then?

I believe that talks with North Korea are largely unsuccessful because the two sides come from two different worlds. We neither speak each other's language nor understand one another's cultures. We interpret each other's actions and intentions from our own perspectives without taking into consideration the other's perspective. It is like we are shooting arrows away from our targets not because we cannot aim but because we're confused about where our targets are.

It is only natural that as outsiders, particularly as Westerners, we do not understand North Korea. It is one of the most reclusive nations on earth. They have been both shut out and closed off from the Western world for approximately seventy years. Therefore, it is amazing that they have remained strong and steadfast despite the fact that much of the world is against them. For this very reason, we cannot assume or expect that North Korea will change any time soon.

The United States often paints North Korea as a volatile nation, completely unpredictable. But if we look at the stance of the nation, what they stand for, and the length of time they have been heading down the same path, we can see that they are, in fact, predictable after all. Perhaps we just do not understand where they are headed, who they are, and for what they stand.

This book is an attempt to pull back the mystery surrounding North Korea and her people.

The information you read in it is based on real experience. It was not learned from other books or academic study. It is an account of first hand experiences and observations gained from over a decade of actually living inside North Korea.

If readers can better understand the North Korean point of view, that understanding will provide context for stories and opinions about North Korea in the mainstream news media. Meaningful peace talks only ever happen on the basis of mutual understanding. To get there we have to be able to come to the negotiating table on an equal footing. The first step towards all of this is simple engagement. Without engagement there cannot be negotiation or peace. As a wise counselor once said, all that is necessary for two parties headed in opposite directions to come together is the willingness to turn and head towards each other.

CHAPTER 1

Where West Meets East

Not very often but occasionally people ask me if I am part Asian.

"Are you sure you don't have any Asian blood in you?" they inquire.

To which I reply, "No, I am one hundred percent Caucasian, from mostly British, Irish, and German descent. But," I add, "it might be my mannerisms that make you think I am part Asian."

Growing up in Asia, I adopted Asian culture into my American heritage. I was born in Canton, Illinois but only because there was no hospital where my family lived. My mother had to travel about twenty minutes by car from our small town of Cuba, Illinois to the hospital in Canton to give birth. Even from the first days of life, my home has been ambiguous. I could not even claim my hometown as my city of birth.

When our family moved to South Korea for my parents to take teaching positions at a small Christian university there, I was only two years old. My father taught Theology and my mother became a Music and Education professor. Growing up in South Korea, I assimilated Korean culture into my identity. At home, we were Americans who celebrated American holidays. My parents were American at heart coming from the Midwestern states of Indiana and Illinois. But every time I stepped outside our home there, I was bombarded by Korean culture.

My greatest shame from my childhood was not learning to speak Korean very well. I attended a Christian international school, so my education was all in English using American curriculum. I studied Korean as a foreign language from elementary all the way through high school but only ever managed to speak survival Korean. I could go shopping and take a taxi, but my conversational vocabulary was severely limited.

Because my Korean was so poor and I was obviously a Caucasian, I felt like I had no right to claim South Korea as my home. Every four years, our family would take a break from life in Korea and spend a year in the United States. One year of my elementary education was spent in Illinois, and one year of middle school in Kentucky. I also spent my junior year of high school in Illinois but returned to Korea for my senior year. After high school graduation, I moved back to the U.S. on my own for college.

By the time I entered college, I had lived in a different location each year of high school. I was a typical "third culture kid" raised in a culture other than my parents', not fully from one or the other, struggling with my own identity. I was a mix of American and Korean culture but ask me where I was from and I had no idea. All I knew was that in my heart I was a mosaic. My Anglo-Saxon outward appearance did not match who I had become on the inside.

When I was fifteen, I discovered a fascination with North Korea. I had begun to read books on the history of Korea and to my surprise, instead of identifying with South Korea, I found I had an affinity for North Korea. One day, I thought, I would work in North Korea. But I was only fifteen, and at the time, North Korea was in the grip of the great famine of the 1990's. Everything in the news about North Korea revolved around two themes: nuclear weapons and a dire shortage of food. I had not heard of anyone visiting or working in North Korea. But I was determined that someday I would go there.

Arriving in the U.S., I began my freshman year at Olivet Nazarene University as a Biology major. Incoming freshmen were asked for their pictures and hometowns to post in the hallway of the Biology Department so that upperclassmen could see the incoming class. Not knowing how to answer the question about my hometown, I put, "Daejeon, Korea".

The only Korean on campus, a young man named Stephen, also happened to be a Biology major. He saw that I had listed my hometown as being from South Korea but was surprised when he looked at the picture and discovered my features. "I have to meet this white, Korean girl," he must have thought. I was on campus only a few weeks when he introduced himself to me.

We discovered that we not only had Biology majors in common but also a desire to work overseas, and so we immediately became friends. Our friendship gradually blossomed into a deeper relationship, and just before our senior year in college we were married. I like to joke that he had no competition. Since Stephen was the only Korean on campus, he was my only choice for a spouse.

When we got married, I thought I had a good understanding of Korean culture. I soon discovered that what I knew at the time was just the tip of the iceberg. My husband was the only son in a Korean family which made him responsible for taking care of his parents as they aged. So after two years of marriage, his parents moved in with us. It was not living with my in-laws that was the real culture shock. After graduation, we moved from Illinois to California. We served at a Korean-American church there while completing our graduate studies. This is where I experienced full immersion into culture shock. The Korean community of Los Angeles taught me about Korean culture on a much deeper level than I'd ever experienced before.

Stephen and I continued to work after graduate school and serve the Korean-American community in Los Angeles. By that time, we had two children. Our daughter was born while I studied for my Master's degree at U.C.L.A., and our son was born soon after graduation. But our desire to work overseas remained in the back of our minds. I still had a heart to go and live in North Korea, something my husband had never considered. Growing up in South Korea, he never imagined it would be possible to go to North Korea.

A conference for Korean-American young adults in 2005 raised our awareness of North Korea. We were just out of graduate school living on entry-level salaries and although I thought it would be splendid for us to attend the conference, we did not have the money. Then we received word of a scholarship which we happily accepted. It was not until we thanked the director of the conference that we discovered there was no such scholarship! The friend who had told us about it had paid directly for our conference fees.

At the conference we met individuals already working in North Korea. There was even a young family living in the Northeast region. Seeing that others were already doing what I had envisioned since I was a teenager caught Stephen's attention. The conference sealed our desire to go work in North Korea. We began making plans to move to Asia. By this time, my husband was about to receive his U.S. citizenship. Once he did, we would be ready to go.

We relocated to South Korea in 2007 in order for me to spend a year in language school. I finally achieved my life-long goal of learning and speaking Korean fluently. It was do or die for me, and I studied with great enthusiasm.

Meanwhile, we began making trips into the Northeast region of North Korea called Rason,[3] a "special economic zone." Our humanitarian work entailed helping rural clinics, kindergartens, and daycare centers. We were told that foreign medical professionals generally do not have the opportunity to treat local people in North Korea, but we got the chance starting the summer of 2007. Our North Korea experience already was surpassing our expectations!

But as is often the case, as major big picture advances were brewing, a tragedy occurred at home. We had just discovered that we were expecting our third child, yet during the one month that Stephen was in North Korea, I miscarried and lost that child.

Since it was early in the pregnancy, we were grateful the miscarriage required no medical intervention. But emotionally, it was one of the most difficult times of my life, and I had to push through it with determination on my own until Stephen returned home.

Moving back to Asia meant yet another level of culture shock for me. For the first time I was expected to behave like a Korean wife and mother. In North Korea, children are considered ethnically Korean if their father is Korean. I was the only non-Korean in the family. This put the pressure on me to conform to Korean culture. I began to realize how American I still was.

Growing up I referred to myself often as a boiled egg. I was white on the outside and yellow (Asian) on the inside, I thought. But the older I got and the more I understood Korean culture, the more I realized that I am not yellow or white. I am both. The combination allows me to see both cultures in depth but remain somewhat objective.

Our year in South Korea led to our family transitioning to Northeast China and eventually into North Korea. Both Stephen and I visited North Korea for the first time together. But because our children were young, I was unable to accompany him much of the time while we were first pioneering our humanitarian presence in North Korea. It took two years of traveling back and forth into North Korea from our base in China before our children were allowed to visit inside with us.

Finally, after a few years of working in North Korea, our family obtained official residency permits for Rason. We stayed in a hotel, homeschooling our children, and continued our medical and humanitarian projects. Most of our humanitarian work involved providing medicine and medical supplies to remote, rural clinics as well as food and educational support for daycares and kindergartens.

Since Stephen was trained as a Chiropractor, he also had the opportunity to treat patients. The majority of his patients included individuals with back injuries or skeletomuscular problems. One day a small five-year old girl with cerebral palsy was brought into the clinic by her grandmother. No one in the region knew how to treat her. Since this girl did not have enough voluntary movement to chew her food, for years her grandmother kept her alive by first chewing the girl's food in her own mouth and then spooning it into her granddaughter's. After just a few treatments, the girl's tone and muscle movement improved. She began moving her fingers and wrapping her arms around her grandmother's shoulders as she was piggy-backed. This little girl changed our family's lives forever.

Even though our humanitarian work in North Korea had just begun, we quickly realized that in order to impact the entire nation of North Korea, we needed a presence in the capital city of Pyongyang. Working in Rason restricted us from traveling outside the special economic zone. An exploratory trip to Pyongyang opened up doors for Stephen to earn a North Korean degree. This local medical doctoral degree would grant him the credentials he would need to routinely treat patients in North Korea.

Stephen began making trips into Pyongyang to study and conduct research for a Ph.D. dissertation. In April of 2012 he earned his doctorate in Rehabilitation Medicine from the DPRK. In most countries, doctoral degrees are conferred by educational institutions. But in North Korea, Ph.D. degrees are only given by the government itself.

His graduation ceremony took place in the State Congressional Building in Pyongyang.

After receiving his degree, our family was invited to the capital city of Pyongyang where Stephen was given a position at Pyongyang Medical School Hospital to train doctors and treat patients on a regular basis. As we prepared to move, our only regret was leaving behind this little girl with cerebral palsy. Who would treat her, we wondered.

Stephen asked the Pyongyang Medical School Hospital Director if the hospital could provide a bed for him to bring her to Pyongyang for treatment. The director was indignant at first. "We don't have cerebral palsy in our country!" he declared. We had no desire to argue with him but we continued to plead for just one hospital bed, and eventually he relented. So it was that through her continued treatment a new program for children with developmental disabilities was born!

Initially, my husband did most of the breadwinning. He was a medical professional. My own expertise was in education. Besides helping him on a regular part-time basis, my time was primarily spent homeschooling our children. When our children were given the opportunity to attend Pyongyang Korean School for Foreigners, my schedule opened up for work on a full-time basis.

The more I observed my husband treating children in the local hospital, the more it burdened me that these children often had to miss months or even years of school while they received treatment. Since we work with children who have developmental disabilities, many of the children had never received an education. I began to look for ways to advocate for their need for education.

After some time, I was eventually able to work directly with children in the hospital. This included providing occupational, speech, and educational therapy. Amazingly, I found myself, an American, teaching North Korean children how to read and write Korean! It was an honoring and humbling experience. I feel privileged to have been entrusted with these children in the hospital.

In recent decades, so much has been written about North Korea by authors who've briefly visited once or twice that focuses on the suffering of the people and on their lack of freedom. Living in North Korea gave me a far more nuanced picture of the realities. Some of it gave details to the sad picture painted by the international press, but other aspects of it surprised me with beauty and hope.

As an American, I did not expect to be well received in North Korea. For example, when I visited the local market each corner I turned in the market was accompanied with giggles and shrills from the female venders. I greeted them in Korean, and several venders would burst out in smiles and laughter. It wasn't all fun and warm. Others looked at me with skepticism. But, many others greeted me with smiles and open hearts. As a result, living in North Korea gave me a broader perspective of the people and a deeper understanding of the country of North Korea. It is this understanding that has broadened my heart for the people of DPRK.

CHAPTER 2

A Different Paradigm

Stepping onto the Air Koryo[4] airplane at the Shenyang airport in China we immediately felt we were in a new world. The flight attendants wore short, red dress suits with a North Korean badge on their left shoulders. They greeted us in both Korean and English.

The flight from Shenyang to Pyongyang was only 45 minutes long, just enough time to take off, serve drinks, and land. Drink options on the flight were either water or North Korean sparkling pear soda. Stephen and I both chose the soda, bottled in glass bottles with a picture of an apple pear on the front. It tasted sweet and had a slight chemical after-taste to it. It was strange and different, but somehow I liked it.

Through our airplane window we caught our first glimpse of the area near Pyongyang. Rice fields interspersed with farm houses and small apartment buildings stretched as far as the eye could see. The airstrip was bordered by a wire fence. Nearby, a farmer with a stick herded a small flock of goats. The city was not yet in view.

As the airplane landed, we could see the expanse of the landing strip. Despite the lack of any air traffic, it took us a good ten minutes to taxi to the main air terminal. Above the two-story building was a sign in large, red Korean letters that read "Pyongyang". We had arrived!

This was not our first visit to North Korea, but it was our first trip to the capital city. Our work in Rason for the past two years providing humanitarian medical aid to clinics and schools had accustomed us to life in the countryside in North Korea, but this was our first taste of life in the capital city.

We had no idea what to expect. We stepped out of the plane onto the stairs and breathed the fresh, crisp autumn air. It was the time of the September Arirang Festival[5], and Stephen and I had brought our three kids with us. Our humanitarian co-workers were also with us on this trip as well as a few other friends. We had come to scope out the land of North Korea. Working in Rason, we could not normally travel outside the special economic zone. Our team knew that if we were to reach out to other parts of the nation, we would need permission from the central government. So, here we were, hoping to learn something about the country and possibly gain new avenues for our humanitarian work.

Our tour guides greeted us at the airport. One older lady in her early fifties and two younger women presumably just out of college stood on the other side of the customs area as we pushed our bags through the X-ray machine. From her authority, it was evident that the older lady was the one in charge and the other two were her subordinates. Short in stature yet having the air of an intellectual woman, she commanded a certain degree of respect. The more time we spent with her the more we could tell that she demanded nothing less than perfection. Yet every once in a while, a smile would break through her stern outward appearance, she would soften, and the warmth of her heart would shine through.

Pyongyang was in the middle of hosting another Arirang Mass Games, an annual cultural spectacle that gives tourists from around the world the opportunity to visit this mysterious city. Our schedule was packed from morning to evening during our entire stay. We were taking full advantage of this trip to see all the major sights in and around the city.

The highlight of the visit of course was the actual Arirang Games, the only performance like it in the world. Tens of thousands of North Korean dancers train for months to perform in perfect unison. Their phased dances tell the story of the nation.

After getting settled in our hotel room, we prepared for the evening's extravaganza. Our entire company loaded into the bus to attend the mass games. All three of our children accompanied us into the arena as we arrived early in the evening before the sun set. Sitting behind us were local North Koreans. They had wisely brought snacks for the evening as the event would go late into the night. We had arrived unprepared to appease our children's hungry appetites. A middle-aged woman reached out her hand and gave our daughter an apple. Here I was, a humanitarian worker, receiving food for my own child from a North Korean lady!

Sitting high in the bleachers on a cool, autumn evening, we waited in anticipation for the performance to begin. Beautiful scenes of ancient Korea unfolded before our eyes. It was serene and peaceful. Then in came the military. A demonstration of the Korean martial art known as Taekwondo portrayed a violent struggle as Japanese invaders subdued an independent Korea. But out of the struggle, one main character emerged. This freedom fighter gathered a constituent to join him in retreating to the mountains.

A fierce snow storm ravaged the mountainside of the sacred mountain Baek-Du. A log cabin appeared. A child was born, and a star came to rest on the mountain as new hope was born into the nation of Korea. One of the two younger guides was sitting next to me. She leaned over and whispered in my ear, "The star is our revolutionary father, the Great Leader. He is going to return to save his people from their oppression."

Suddenly, from the storm emerged a calm. The star, shining brighter than ever before, flew off in the distance to return to its homeland. The scene changed from a somber mood to a time of celebration. The star returned. The people were saved. Freedom from oppression gave them reason to rejoice!

Dancing followed more dancing. Rhythmic gymnastics were performed to a level of excellence that was almost creepy. The storyline continued to unfold: the country flourished with scientific advancements and abundant farm produce. Life was good.

What does this mean? I wondered to myself as I watched. I tried to digest everything our guide was whispering in my ear during the performances. One thing was clear. This was the history of the North Korean people in epic form and very central to it was the story of their hero, the bright star, their founding leader, Kim Il-Sung.

That first trip into Pyongyang was enlightening but also exhausting. Never before had I been so immersed in such an intense culture. Our family enjoyed our brief stay in Pyongyang thoroughly, but it took a good week for us to recover physically from our visit. Our exhaustion was not just from the travel and the busy tour schedule but also from the experience of overwhelming indoctrination by North Korean propaganda.

North Korea is set apart from the rest of the world, we realized. It is not just about being isolated from the international community but also about their unique paradigm. Their understanding and interpretation of historical events and their world perspective is different from anything we had ever experienced. Whether they are right or wrong, we felt we should try to understand their paradigm of the world. What is it that they understand and believe? What is their interpretation of history? How do they see themselves in relation to the rest of the world?

At the end of our trip, we were surprised by an invitation to return to Pyongyang. As we were leaving at the airport, the senior guide said to us, "I would like you to come back. Please write a letter to our government requesting that you return to Pyongyang. This time, I would like you to come and provide the medical services you have been providing in the Northeast Region. Our country can use you."

Never in a million years would we have guessed that this was to be the start of a long journey into the heart of North Korea. Our insights into the nation were just beginning. As we would later move to live in the city of Pyongyang, we had limitless lessons yet to learn.

CHAPTER 3

In Their Own Eyes

Our family began transitioning to live in Pyongyang. We relocated to the city during the April 15th Holiday, the largest holiday of the year which is the birthday of Kim Il-Sung. Along with our three children, we were planning on living the entire spring semester in the capital to develop our Spine Rehabilitation Center at the Pyongyang Medical School Hospital. Since the kids were with us, it was quite challenging homeschooling and participating in holiday events all at the same time. Thankfully, our minder, or guide as we like to call him, liked children.

Our first guide was a gentle older man who enjoyed connecting with our kids. He had two teenaged daughters himself, so he had our children call him uncle, a common way for children to address older men in N.K. This man taught us the role guides in North Korea were to play in our daily life in Pyongyang for the next five years, and he became an uncle to our children.

One Sunday afternoon while we were resting at home, I couldn't find our youngest daughter.

Being about four years-old at the time, she was always getting into a lot of mischief, so I wasn't surprised that she had wandered off. I eventually found her in the back room behind the kitchen where only local grounds keepers were allowed. She was playing doctor on our guide. He lay on the floor with his shirt rolled up to his chest as our daughter listened to his "heart beat" with her toy stethoscope. He didn't seem to mind, even though she was interrupting his Sunday afternoon nap!

Local guides or "interpreters" are an ever-present part of the life of every foreigner in North Korea. All foreigners are required to have them. They act as our business associates for all the work that we do there. The guides are responsible for several things. First, their primary job is to escort us around the city and instruct us on appropriate behavior and customs. They are also there to protect us from harm. As our representation to locals in North Korea, they will defend us and advocate for us in the event we are criticized or wrongly accused. Second, they are responsible for arranging our schedule including business meetings with our local business counterparts. And of course, last but not least, they report back to the government on all our activities. Essentially what this means is that if our project is a success, they themselves are perceived favorably by their own government.

So much of our time in North Korea was spent with our guide that we learned to invest in the relationship. It became clear that our guide could make or break our work in the country. A good relationship could open roads to new opportunities and help us succeed even in the midst of challenging circumstances. A poor relationship could lead to being expelled from the country, or worse.

Whenever we had somewhere to go that involved travel outside of our town, we would dine on the road with our guide and whomever else we might be meeting with that day. We also ate meals together as part of our work day at home. And so it was that over meals we often found ourselves discussing interesting topics with our official representatives in a way that didn't happen at any other point of our working relationship.

One day at the end of the work week in Pyongyang, Stephen and the kids and I and our local guide as well as our driver were all eating together at a local restaurant. Eating out is expensive in Pyongyang, so we usually reserved only one day a week for a meal out on the weekend. As the work for the week was finished and we were relaxing over a few drinks and appetizers, we waited for the main meal to arrive. Our kids were busy playing games and watching the restaurant's television. It was a cozy atmosphere as we chatted and watched Russian figure skating on the flat screen T.V.

By this point in our experience in North Korea, I had had opportunity to observe our interaction with our guides quite a bit. What I had noticed was that our conversations over meals tended to begin with a light tone and center on nothing more personal or involved than work-related issues. But on this occasion, we began to discuss the Korean people. Since I had done some personal study of Korean history we began comparing notes on who the Korean people were and from whence they had come.

I mentioned my study of Korean history to our guide and we began to freely discuss it. As far as I understood, I said, the Korean people were a tribal people descended from the Mongolians. Like the Mongolians, I noted, Koreans have an Altaic[6] culture and language. Also, genetic research has shown that Koreans are most closely related to Mongolians followed by the Japanese. This research described the Korean nation migrating from the Lake of Baikal in Russia, which is located just north of Mongolia.[7] Linguistically, I went on, Korean is distantly related to Turkish, as well as Mongolian, Japanese, and other Altaic languages. According to this historical evidence, I concluded, it is generally assumed that Korean tribes migrated into the Korean Peninsula approximately 5,000 years ago, settled and became the agricultural Korean nation we know today.

As I described my research and knowledge of ancient Korean origins, our local counterpart became increasingly agitated. Finally, he could contain himself no longer. "Koreans are not related to any other people!" he emphatically exclaimed. "We are our own race and people! We did not come from Mongolians!"

Our conversation abruptly changed direction. Our guide explained that Koreans were descended from their ancient forefather Dangun. I listened to him in surprise and wondered what he himself truly believed. We finished dinner rather quietly as we picked up the tab and returned home.

According to Korean folklore, I knew that the Korean people were descended from Dangun the grandson of Hwan-in the "Lord of Heaven". Hwan-in's son Hwan-ung, came down to earth and landed on a sacred mountain in order to marry an earthly woman who then gave birth to their son Dangun.[8]

The woman Hwan-ung married was no ordinary woman either. As the story goes, a tiger and a bear came to Hwan-ung asking him to make them human. Hwan-ung gave them each a bundle of a bitter root and told them to live in a cave for 100 days surviving on nothing but this bundle of bitter root. In the end, the animal that was able to endure the 100 days would become human. The tiger did not last 100 days, but the bear did and was transformed into the human woman Ungnyeo. Hwan-ung and Ungnyeo gave birth to Dangun who became the founder of the Korean peoples.[9] Dangun was said to have united the nine wild tribes of Korea.

Although I was familiar with this animistic mythical account of the origin of Korea, I never imagined it might be the mainstream understanding in North Korea. But as I talked with my local counterpart, I found that it was exactly that. I began to understand the depth of the fierce sense of national pride and ethnic identity all Koreans share. North Koreans really do believe that they are a unique race on this earth. Their mythology emphasizes direct relations to the "Lord of Heaven". To suggest to a Korean that they are related to Mongolians is an insult to the very core of their identity.

North Korea, in particular, has emphasized the mythical origins of all of Korea. Certain mountains are sacred to the Korean people. Their leaders are divinely appointed. This has spurred on the group culture and ethnocentric thinking in Korea as well as fueled their national pride. To a North Korean, the main purpose for living is to fight for, preserve, and protect the Korean nation.

Dangun is not entirely only a mythological figure. Dangun is recorded historically as the first king of the Korean people who ruled Korea during the Gojoseon Dynasty starting around the year of 2,333 B.C.[10] His grave still exists today about a twenty minutes' drive outside the city of Pyongyang. North Korea celebrates National Foundation Day each year on October 3rd, which is a commemoration of Dangun.

In 2015, during our third year in Pyongyang, our family had the privilege of attending the celebration of the founding of Korea. The event was broadcast nationally, as such holidays are in North Korea. The ceremony took place at the tomb of Dangun and began with reverent offerings presented in the traditional Confucian way, which is respectful of one's ancestors. Offerings of fruit, nuts, rice cakes, and vegetables were spread across a limestone altar in front of the pyramid-shaped tomb. Burning incense completed the sacred offering. Although the ceremony was rather simple and short by North Korean standards, after the speeches every Korean in attendance bowed in reverent respect to their founding king.

Afterwards we were able to stroll through the inner maze of the tomb itself. The entire tomb is built with large slabs of limestone, stacked to create a dome-like pyramid. The inside of the tomb is rather simple. I expected something opulent and ornate, perhaps a little more like the tomb of King Tut. But there were no treasures or even a grand casket. All we saw was an ancient painting of Dangun placed at the entrance to what was apparently his final resting place.

The fact that the tomb lacks grandeur made it feel more authentic somehow. Rooted deep in history, this mythical god-son Dangun, was in fact the real founder of the Korean nation. And the place of his capital city was no other than Pyongyang itself.

The Koreans at the ceremony quietly went through obligatory motions of respect as they often do at these ceremonies. I could tell that their level of passion for Dangun was nowhere near their level of enthusiasm for their current leader. Despite their lack of energy, it was transparently clear that the Korean people have deep, ancient roots. They have remained a predominantly mono-ethnic and mono-cultural people for approximately 5,000 years.

Perhaps the best explanation of the Korean peoples, though, is found in their self-declared name, the "Arirang People". "Arirang" is the title of the single, most ancient song of Korean culture. It is so ancient that no one knows the true meaning of the word "arirang". Yet the song is deeply engraved in the hearts of every Korean, whether from North or South.

The "Arirang" song is sung and played just about everywhere in Korea. Both North and South Korea have various versions and editions of the song. Restaurants are named after the song as well as shops, books, hotels, and just about anything pertaining to Korean culture. The annual Mass Games performed in Pyongyang are referred to as the "Arirang Mass Games", which is only fitting because the entire event revolves around the identity of the Korean people.

However, the lyrics to "Arirang" are as mysterious as the mythical origins of Korea, herself. Many historians have explained the meaning of the song, but still to this day, there is no single one take that is universally accepted as the only interpretation. The song's meaning changes over time to reflect the changing heart of the nation.

A rough translation of the lyrics might go as follows:

Arirang, arirang, a-la-lee-o
Arirang, we travel over the hills
You desert me, you are leaving me
Your feet will be sore even before you travel ten li (5 km)
Yet, we travel on...

Clearly it speaks to the pain and the suffering of the Korean people. It talks of Korea's weariness and tiresome journey. Yet despite the obstacles of the terrain, the Korean people press forward. Even though they may lose some of their own through the cruelty of the journey, they will forge on. They will never give up. They sing of their suffering as each urges the others to persevere.

This epitomizes the character of the Koreans. They are a fiercely determined people. No matter what the cost, how much the pain and suffering, or how much the loss, they will not give up. Why? Because they are a proud, mono-ethnic people with 5,000 years of history, and they will do anything and everything to preserve their nation. They are the "Arirang People."

CHAPTER 4

Unique Historical Perspectives

After a few months, life in the big city settled into a routine. In the mornings the children and I homeschooled, and then I filled the afternoons with fun activities for the kids and an occasional trip to the hospital with my husband. Since I was busy homeschooling during my early years in North Korea, my main responsibilities were administrative duties that I could do from home as well as cooking for our team. Every evening, team members would return from the hospital to a home-cooked meal ready to devour the minute they walked in the door. Evenings were filled with debriefing over the progress of our project and preparing the next day's sack lunch for work. There was never a dull moment in community life as we shared our accommodations in North Korea with our entire team.

During our first two years in the Northeast region, things had been different. The whole family often accompanied Stephen on trips to clinics and kindergartens in remote fishing and farming villages. But in the city, the kids did not have many opportunities to "go to work" with their father since we worked at the most elite, tertiary hospital in the nation. Our daily schedule was only interrupted by verification trips for large donations of food, clothing, and medicine. I often visited orphanages for this reason. One thing that struck me through these visits was the extent to which North Korea was impacted by its history.

In any history book from either North or South Korea, readers will find descriptions of the invasions and attacks on Korea by neighboring countries. Koreans today will often say that over the span of their 5,000 some years of history, Korea was invaded by China (Manchuria), Mongolia, and Japan numerous times.[11] But as described by Andrei Lankov, these attacks were primarily in the past one hundred years, and do not necessarily describe the whole of Korean history.[12] Also important to note is that despite these attacks, Korea was rarely completely occupied by a foreign entity.[13] For the most part, Korea fought off foreign invasions. It wasn't until the Japanese occupation from 1910 to 1945 that Korea was completely subdued by an outside power.

In response to this experience, the predominant foreign policy during the final Korean dynasty, the Joseon (Chosun) Dynasty, was isolationism,

"Hermit Nation" status.[14] This policy was meant to protect the country from foreign invasion and occupation and from that perspective, it served its purpose. For nearly 200 years, the nation escaped invasion.

North Korea perpetuates the Joseon Dynasty mentality, as reflected in their name "Chosun"[15]. Since their formation in 1948, they've continued the policy of international isolation from the Joseon era. In their minds, foreign influence can only lead to foreign rule. They are convinced that the more foreign influence Korea accepts, the weaker and more susceptible she is to losing her roots and returning to being the foreign-dominated, colonized country she was during the much-hated Japanese Occupation.

This concept is often hard for Westerners to understand because it touches on one of the main differences between socialist and democratic societies: focus on the past versus the future. Although this is a generalization, it is a key aspect of North Korean culture that is worth noting. Socialist countries tend to be collectivistic or group cultures, whereas democratic countries lean toward individualism. As a result, most socialist cultures place greater emphasis on history in order to identify with the formation of the people group and nation. The past very much defines who the group is and where they are headed. Contrastingly, since democratic countries are predominately individualistic, their cultures focus on the future. We think, "The past is in the past". We are the authors of our own destinies. Therefore, we should focus on the future, and not the past.

This fundamental cultural difference leads to huge misunderstandings between socialist and democratic countries. Westerners, typically being democratic, may comment on Asian socialist countries as being "stuck in the past", while for Asians, the past is what defines their identity as a people.

Like many other Asian people groups, the whole of Korea focuses primarily on the past. There are specific distinctions however, between which aspects of history are emphasized by the North and which are emphasized by the South. Although schools in both North and South Korea study the entire expanse of Korean history from ancient to modern times, the two countries emphasize different parts of the story. For instance, North Korea emphasizes the period of the Koryeo Dynasty, whereas South Korea emphasizes the Shilla Dynasty. The Koryeo Dynasty was primarily a northern dynasty that claimed Pyongyang as its capital. The Shilla Dynasty was of greater importance to South Korea because at that time the Korean Peninsula was broken into three kingdoms with two kingdoms in the south and one in the north.[16] In the same way that North and South Korea differentiate between their ancient pasts, they have different accounts of modern history.

In North Korea, modern history focuses on the Japanese occupation and the liberation of Korea after World War II leading to the establishment of the Democratic Peoples' Republic of Korea and the Kim leadership. In particular, North Korea focuses on the painful destruction of their nation in the Korean War. I have personally seen how North Koreans have been extremely traumatized by the bombing, destruction, and ravaging of their nation from 1950 to 1953.[17]

I was unaware of the depth of North Korea's trauma until I witnessed their depictions of the Korean War. As I often visited orphanages, kindergartens, and childcare facilities in North Korea, I caught a glimpse into how the war is affecting the current generation. Orphanages house kids from ages five to sixteen, and daycare and kindergarten facilities care for children from three months to four years. Without exception, almost every childcare center I visited has pictures of the Korean

War on the walls of their hallways. These pictures may be replicas of actual photographs or they may just be murals painted on the walls. Either way, they provide examples of the suffering and inhumane treatment of their people by U.S. and U.N. forces during the Korean War. Some pictures are of war scenes and gruesome fights. Other photographs are of dead bodies and mass graves and are comparable to the photographs I have viewed of the Jewish Holocaust. Every child in North Korea grows up viewing these pictures on a daily basis. It was through these pictures in childcare facilities and schools that I realized how deeply traumatized North Koreans were by the war.

It may appear at first glance that these pictures are just another example of the state's propaganda. But how is this information shaping the hearts and minds of children in North Korea? In North Korea, it can be difficult to distinguish between propaganda and truth. However, there is no doubt that the Korean War, though it lasted only three years, was one of the most brutal wars ever fought.[18] Approximately 400,000 bombs were dropped on the capital city Pyongyang alone, and at the time, the population of Pyongyang was only 400,000.[19] That means that one bomb was dropped for each person living in the city. Inyeop Lee states that twenty percent of the North Korean population was killed in the Korean War.[20]

Sixty-five years after the end of hostilities, North Korea is still digging up live ordnance in their country left from the war. The twenty-two cities that existed in North Korea at the time were all demolished in the war.[21] To put this in perspective, the number of bombs dropped on North Korea during the Korean War was roughly the same as the number of bombs dropped on Japan during World War II.[22] But since the DPRK has a much smaller geographical area, there were more bombs dropped on North Korea per square meter than on Japan in World War II, even though North Korea was never attacked with a nuclear bomb. According to Talmadge, North Korea is estimated to be the second most bombed nation in our entire world history![23] Cambodia is the only nation in the world that was bombed more, sadly.[24]

In the United States, the Korean Conflict has been written off in textbooks as the "Forgotten War".[25] It has been overshadowed by larger World Wars and the more recent war against terrorism as well as the controversial Vietnam War. Younger generations in America have little knowledge of the Korean Conflict. What we do read about the Korean War in the West is lacking in detail, at least from a North Korean point of view. Of all things, the most common characteristic of the war described in history books is the weather: the bitter, cold winters of Korea! While U.S. History emphasizes the weather in Korea, the fact is that approximately 1 million North Koreans were killed in the war and roughly 600,000 of them were civilians.[26]

The memory of the war is still fresh and alive for North Koreans, kept so by yearly national remembering and commemoration. Besides murals and depictions in schools, hospitals, orphanages and other public buildings in North Korea, there are several large museums and memorials dedicated entirely to the Korean War. In the capital city of Pyongyang, there is a newly built, vast museum to the Korean War as well as a memorial to those who gave their lives in the war. In contrast, in South Korea, the War Memorial of Korea in Seoul only has a single exhibit hall dedicated to the Korean War. Other exhibits are dedicated to battles fought throughout the rest of Korean history.

In the spring of 2014, our family had the privilege of touring the Korean War Museum shortly after its opening. The building is enormous, built of limestone and granite and divided into two sections. One section is for the main exhibits. The second building is connected by a walkway and consists of a domed structure housing a virtual experience of the Battle of Daejeon.

The museum surprised me. I was expecting violent depictions of war, but for the most part the displays avoided gruesome details. Instead, the main objective of the museum is the tyranny of American imperialism. U.S. soldiers are depicted in exaggerated postures of utter defeat, some holding crosses on chains or even clutching Bibles. It is as if North Korea is likening the U.S. defense of South Korea to the Crusades in the Dark Ages. The propaganda of the state of North Korea declares that as a Christian nation, the United States intended to take over North Korea primarily to serve their own political gain. Americans and Christians are lumped together, sharing the purpose of the advancement of Western civilization. At the end of the exhibit, North Korea heroically prevails over their enemies, victoriously fighting off the foreign invaders.

North Korea clearly has their own take on the Korean War. It is true that the war was never formally ended. Instead, hostilities ceased by signing an armistice. North Korea portrays the war as their victory over the imperialistic powers that sought to overtake them, but they are also keenly aware that it is officially unfinished. Because of that, joint military exercises between the U.S. and South Korea along the border with North Korea are a highly sensitive matter.

In almost every workplace in North Korea there are banners that read, “This is a War Zone”. The country spurs their people on to work as if they are fighting for their lives and the preservation of their nation. The people of North Korea have been conditioned to be ready for an attack from the United States at any moment. They are determined not to ever again allow their country to lie in ruins or their people to be massacred as they were in the Korean War.

CHAPTER 5

North Korea's Worldview

One of the biggest misconceptions about the government and people of North Korea is that they do not want to engage with the world. Multiple times acquaintances have been shocked to hear that we have lived and worked in North Korea. At least a dozen times someone has asked, "But aren't you American? How could you go into North Korea as a U.S. citizen? Is it allowed?"

My reply before the U.S. travel ban was always the same. "Yes, it's allowed and even encouraged to a certain degree. The only countries whose citizens are unable to visit North Korea due to restrictions imposed by North Korea are Israel and, for the most part, South Korea." Only with special permission from both governments can South Koreans also visit North Korea. Governmental delegations from South Korea *have* visited Pyongyang on several occasions. Ordinary South Korean citizens cannot travel to North Korea though, because of the political and diplomatic discord between the two countries. In the case of Israeli visitors, I assume that North Korea's close economic and military ties with Israel's enemies among Middle Eastern Islamic nations has kept North Korea from allowing Israeli tourists.[27]

Certainly, visiting North Korea is not like going to Canada or England from the U.S. For instance, by simply looking at our passports it is hard to prove that we have even been there at all. Since the U.S. does not have normal diplomatic relations with North Korea, Americans cannot officially have a North Korean immigration stamp in our passports. Instead, the border personnel insert a temporary visa page on which all official stamps are placed. If someone were to inspect our passport without that page, they would only see that we have entered and exited China numerous times with no indication that North Korea was our final destination.

When Stephen and I began working in North Korea, we entered the country through a border crossing into the northernmost region Rason. Rason, known simply as the Northeast Region to locals, is a Special economic zone, one of few designated areas in the country where North Korea encourages business engagement with the world. Foreigners traveling to that area are able to obtain invitations in a relatively simple fashion without having to apply for a visa at a North Korean Embassy. In order to enter this zone, one need only send a one-page application to the North Korean Special Economic Zone Business Bureau. Invitation inserts serve as visa-like papers and are picked up on-site at immigration as one enters the country at the border.

Special economic zones are where North Korea is testing opening their borders to the rest of the world. They are testing the waters for international business and experimenting to see the benefits to their economy by opening their society to interaction with an international community.[28]

Living and working in Rason had certain advantages over living and working in Pyongyang. Initially, as in Pyongyang, all foreigners are escorted by local guides. But after a vetting period ranging from a few months to a few years, foreigners in Rason may apply for and obtain foreign resident cards and then local guides are no longer needed. In comparison to Pyongyang, where only foreign diplomats and their staff can obtain resident cards, there is relative freedom for foreigners in Rason.

Be that as it may, everywhere you go in Rason, as with the rest of the country, you will see the same government slogans on banners, posters and billboards placed in visible locations in every public space. The bureaucracy may apply policies more leniently in order to encourage foreign investment, but the area is still very much a region of North Korea. In short, it is still under the control of the central government and governed by all the same laws.

Slogans such as "Let's Do It Our Way", "One Heart, One Mind", and "Even if the Road is Difficult, Let's Laugh as We Go!" are plastered everywhere. Although North Korea is making attempts to slowly open up to the international community, they are unwilling to compromise on their way of doing things.

Rason is actually a rather small rural area. Because fewer people live there and because it is a special economic zone, it is much more common to see foreigners in Rason than it is even in Pyongyang despite the fact that the embassies of Russia, China, and Iran, the three largest foreign embassies in North Korea, are located in Pyongyang. In the city, one might see Russians freely walking around on the streets, especially in the central part of town where their embassy is located. And tour buses full of foreign visitors travel around the city, stopping at the most popular sight-seeing spots, escorted everywhere they go by their teams of guides and interpreters. But in Rason, one would run into other foreigners in the market or in the street and it was clear that they were 'local' foreigners who lived and worked there.

It impressed me to learn that North Korea provides interpreters in all of the most common foreign languages for every single visiting tourist and diplomat. The educated class of North Korea does a great job of mastering foreign languages. True their language schools emphasize listening to recordings since live interaction with foreign language speakers during their education is so limited. But an educated North Korean often speaks up to three languages the most common being Russian, Chinese, Japanese, German and of course English.

North Koreans are avid students of foreign language, partly to gain opportunities for study abroad. Despite the fact that in one sense North Korea continues to isolate itself from the world, North Koreans today are also increasingly actively engaged with other friendly nations. North Koreans now not only study abroad when the opportunity is provided by the governments concerned but they also work abroad. Hundreds of thousands of North Koreans work in Russia, China, Cambodia, the Middle East, and certain African countries.[29] They most commonly work as unskilled laborers, painters, construction workers, loggers, even restaurant or hotel staff.

While working or studying abroad, their interaction with their host countries is limited. North Koreans never travel alone, always in groups. In these groups, they keep each other accountable to not become "polluted" by the world's capitalistic thinking. When they return home after a few years, they get re-educated before returning to work.

Clearly, even though the North Korean government seeks to engage with the world for economic benefit, whether through special economic zones or exporting workers overseas, they are careful not to allow any of their citizens to deviate from the official ways of thinking. In fact, official North Korea would rather forego all foreign investment than give up the North Korean way of life.

On an unofficial level however, there is growing desire in North Korea to interact with the world. People we met were eager to receive news from the outside world. To address this growing sentiment in the population, North Korean television and radio are broadcasting more and more international news all the time.

Skeptics of course question whether North Korea genuinely wants to engage with the outside world, or whether they merely covet the material benefits of open international relations on their own terms. This inherent conflict is one of the things that makes it difficult for North Korea to fully open itself to the world.

Over time, we came to the conviction that North Korea does genuinely appreciate respectful interaction with foreign countries. For my first birthday in North Korea, we visited the famous Myohyang Mountain just north of Pyongyang. Although Myohyangsan is not one of the larger mountains in Korea, it is appreciated for its scenic beauty and the historic mythical significance of being the home of Dangun. While we were there we had the option of taking several hiking paths to explore the area, but we opted instead to have a simple picnic along a stream that ran down the mountainside. It was a refreshing and relaxing atmosphere in the middle of a mixed forest of sweet smelling deciduous and coniferous trees. Sitting in the sunshine on the banks of an ice-cold mountain stream on the side of the mountain, we ate our box lunches of rice with side dishes of meat and vegetables and sang impromptu karaoke. It was a beautiful moment that I'll never forget.

After our picnic, we visited the nearby museums that host the gifts from foreign nations given to the Kim family. Two large Confucian style buildings housed gifts from all over the world including nations in Africa, Asia, and Europe, and even some from the United States. Hallways upon hallways displayed thousands of gifts from every corner of the earth.[30]

Another special section of the museum was dedicated to the honorary doctorates and degrees presented to the Founding Leader. South American nations, African nations, and even some European nations had offered the Kim Leader medals, plaques, degrees, and doctoral robes. To say that the museum was overwhelming is putting it mildly!

The number of countries that had sent visitors to the Great Leader was presented visually through documentaries that played one after the other on screens located throughout. International leaders had apparently come one after another to pay their respects and offer gifts of friendship. And on occasion, the North Korean leader himself was hosted abroad by some of these various nations.

It wasn't until later, after the collapse of the Soviet Union and the fall of the Iron Curtain, that North Korea found itself so completely isolated from the world. From the early 1960's to 1970's, North Korea's economy was stronger than the South's. During the communist "golden era," North Korea traded regularly with friendly nations. Annual international conferences were held with

Heads of State from these countries at a special conference center built in 1980 on the west side of Pyongyang.

Today North Korea has far fewer options for international relations. Their closest allies are Russia and China, but the support of those nations is not always reliable or predictable. Russia and China have to weigh consequences imposed by the U.N. and the United States.

For several years[31], the Arirang Mass Games were performed annually in Pyongyang. These mass games gave the country a means to present the nation's agenda for each year in an entertaining fashion. Our family tried to attend the Mass Games every year while we were there. It was great entertainment, and it gave us insight into the political strategic objectives for each year.

In 2013, we witnessed a significant change in the Mass Games routine. In previous years the program had consisted of historic components followed by dramatized statements of the central government's political goals for the year. Artistically, themes had also revolved around the national focus of the year. However, the organizers added a new component in 2013. North Korea used the Mass Games that year to specifically promote their international relations with China. A special friendship with China was presented through the dance routines. Chinese dancers in traditional Chinese red costumes danced hand-in-hand with North Korean performers around a lotus flower that represented the fruitful friendship between the two countries.

CHAPTER 6
Juche

In the early days in Rason, it felt as though Stephen and I and our colleagues from the humanitarian organization were going into a war zone every single day. Day by day we battled local officials to make sure our work was done transparently. We argued intensely over details like monitoring and appropriate use and allocation of humanitarian goods. We entered North Korea each time thinking that the North Korean officials we would deal with were simply not to be trusted. They were there to cheat us for what they wanted, or so we thought. We had been warned that we should be careful about bribes and to be on our guard against officials manipulating our work for their own personal gain.

It was exhausting arguing with our North Korean counterparts! We were there to serve the common, local person and to provide food and medical care to the least privileged. Was it worth it to go through this battle every day? Did our humanitarian assistance even matter, we wondered?

As we grew to know the North Korean officials,

though, we began to feel that maybe they were really concerned about their fellow countrymen. True, they were confined by a system that did not allow much leeway, but we began to wonder if maybe, just maybe, their hearts were in the right place. So, after talking about it, we took a leap of faith. We decided we would start trusting our North Korean counterparts. To our amazement, the more we trusted them, the greater the opportunities opened for us to do the work that we were there to do.

We soon discovered that what really enabled us to build trust with the officials we worked with was to spend time with them. Outside of the confines of work, we began to make an effort to eat meals with our North Korean counterparts, even though we quickly also discovered that we would have to foot the bill every time. During down times, we would play billiards with the officials and even visit the local hot springs spa together. We found that through spending quality time together we were finally able to catch glimpses of their own daily lives, glimpses that revealed their personal opinions and their everyday thought processes.

We found that North Koreans are culturally Korean at heart, but distinguished from their southern brethren by their "Juche" philosophy.

The Juche Philosophy is the worldview for all North Koreans and the foundational ideology of their Communist Party. Written by their founding leader Kim Il-Sung, it is the code by which every North Korean citizen must live.

Juche has been approximately translated into English as "self-reliance." It teaches the ability to stand on one's own abilities and strength. It is human-focused in all of its tenets. Rather than demoralizing people, it actually emphasizes the value of human worth and effort, especially collective human worth and effort, effort united in large groups or masses.

There are three main tenets of Juche: creativity, consciousness, and self-reliance. Self-reliance in turn has three areas of expression.[32] The first is political independence, the second economic self-sustenance, and the third self-reliance in defense.[33] Each of the tenets form a part of North Korea's political objectives and policies, whether domestic, foreign or military. North Korea's overriding objective is to be self-sufficient in all aspects of national and personal life.

Besides the national political arena, Juche is lived out by the nation's citizens in daily life. The people of North Korea model their actions and behavior after the Juche philosophy, from their personal work ethnic to their daily decision-making process.

During our first two years living in Rason, doing humanitarian work and social entrepreneurship, we needed to travel throughout the region by car. Part of our work was to directly service all of the rural clinics, kindergartens, and daycare centers that we supported. We delivered rice, cooking oil, and medicines to remote fishing and farming villages. From the main city, we would often spend half a day on the road just to get to the village we were visiting that day. Roads in North Korea are not great. Only a few of the main roads are actually paved and the dirt local roads were impassible whenever snow or heavy rains fell. An entire road might be flooded or washed out by the weather. Driving was always slow. Pot holes were common everywhere and so we had to drive slowly or risk damaging our vehicle.

Since the bulk of our work was making deliveries of food and medicine, after the first two years we purchased our own truck to transport the precious supplies. The truck had limited seating so we would travel in two vehicles, one just for people and the other for the supplies and any remaining passengers. In very remote settings, we even had to travel where there were no roads. In those cases we would drive right through the rice paddies or along a creek bed to get to the village.

On one such occasion, our vehicle got stuck in the middle of a creek. It was in the winter when temperatures in North Korea can get down to minus thirty degrees Celsius. The stream was frozen, and the only way across was over the ice. Our vehicle made it half-way across, and then broke through the ice and got hopelessly stuck. No amount of effort would free the wheels from the imprisonment of the stream.

People from the village, including children, came out to survey our situation. What did they do? They proceeded to burn fires to melt the ice. Then, one of them arrived with a farm tractor to pull our vehicle out of the frozen ice. It took some time, but eventually we crossed that stream and got to the other side!

With self-reliance comes a special creativity. Since people are taught to rely upon no one else, they find ingenious ways to solve problems. People are taught to be self-sufficient in circumstances that would normally require outside assistance.

Professional drivers in North Korea all double as mechanics. Not only do they know how to drive their vehicle, but also how to fix and maintain it. Our truck broke down frequently and there are not many car repair shops in North Korea. But we found that there was no need for any! Our driver, being the creative mechanic that he is, fixed our car with few tools. And his most valuable tool was a paper clip!

Ironically, self-reliance also teaches a philosophy of independence, which hinders the spirit of cooperation. One way this is demonstrated is in departments in North Korea acting in self-sufficiency. Communication between departments is lacking. Each sector is expected to creatively solve problems on their own.

While the West now emphasizes cooperative learning and joint task forces, East Asia is emphasizing "survival of the fittest". Competition is intense, and only the best become successful.

This poses a challenge when working within a North Korean company. Instead of local workers helping us resolve problems, they will try to fix the problem on their own. It takes considerable effort for us to convince them to share challenging issues with us. But once we are able to overcome that obstacle, we find that we can work together towards resolution. Their self-reliance indoctrination makes it difficult to work in unison, but once we find a way to cooperate, they discover that together our creativity is multiplied exponentially!

North Koreans feel that it is their creativity and self-reliance that has allowed them to survive years of sanctions. Self-reliance has even stopped them from asking for help from the nations around them. Most of North Korea's economic assistance has come from Communist or former Communist nations, mainly China. North Korea is open to receiving help from China because they feel that China understands their communist ideals and socialist way of life.

CHAPTER 7

A Mile in Their Shoes

Daily life in North Korea can differ vastly depending upon where one lives and works. Regardless of position in life, one thing is sure, North Koreans, like many Koreans everywhere, are industrious almost to a fault.

In some ways, our life as foreigners in North Korea was more relaxed than theirs. In other ways, we had more challenges. Our work day was shorter for instance, as well as our work week. On the other hand, when we went home every day our work was not finished. We had communications and project reports to write for our NGO board members back home. We also had more restrictions and limitations placed on us as foreigners, so that even small things like going grocery shopping were complicated. Our understanding of their daily lives is only through glimpses, but we do have some idea from our limited experience what it means to be North Korean.

In Pyongyang work began at nine o'clock. We would leave our home at precisely twenty minutes past eight to travel to the hospital. Our children started their school day at the Korean School for Foreigners at eight forty-five. After dropping them off at school, we needed at least forty minutes to get to the hospital. Gas stations are scarce in the city and since the best prices were in the vicinity of the kids' school, we would sometimes have to add extra time to our travel to stop for gas on our way.

When we arrived at the hospital, our North Korean counterparts were already there. Our guide would always call in advance to make sure that they would be waiting for us at the hospital entrance the moment our car pulled up. Everywhere we went in the hospital, we were escorted by the foreign liaison. But once we arrived at our treatment room, our Rehabilitation Department colleagues would take responsibility for us. Several hours each morning and afternoon were then spent treating patients and training doctors through hands-on therapy.

Without exception, lunch in North Korea (everywhere, not just in our hospital) was a two-hour break. It allowed for some leisure, eating and chatting over our simple meal of cold noodles. Occasionally in the coldest months, cold noodles would be replaced with hot corn noodles. Only for special occasions and guests is the lunch menu ever changed. The typical daily meal was a bowl of buckwheat noodles with a few pieces of radish, spicy pickled cabbage (kimchi), and half an egg.

A two-hour lunch gave us time to check email, work on our project reports, and sometimes even take a short nap. For most people, two hours was what they needed to travel home for lunch and then return back to their school or workplace. Two hours may sound like a lot of time when some workplaces in the West provide only thirty minutes for lunch. But having lived in North Korea and experienced daily life there, in some ways, two hours is not enough.

Most people walk to school or work. Some in large cities have the privilege of public transportation. This might include buses, street cars, or even subway (metro). Lines on public transportation though, are long and slow. It's not unusual for a person to travel thirty minutes to an hour or more to reach their place of work.

Once they arrive home, if there is not a full-time housekeeper in the family, they have to cook. Otherwise, extra hours in the morning are required to make both breakfast and extra food for a boxed lunch of rice and side dishes. Cooking rice is not simple. The outer husk of the rice grain called chaff, is still separated from harvested rice in North Korea the old-fashioned way, by throwing the grain up in the air and beating it on the ground with straw brooms. As a result, there are often small rocks in the rice from this winnowing process. The upshot is that one must always sift one's rice before cooking it.

North Koreans are experts at sifting rice, but when we got there we were not. The first few times I tried, it took me about an hour each time to sift the rice before cooking a meal. That was just the sifting time. Add the other prep and cooking time and each meal took no less than two hours to fully prepare! North Koreans prepare their rice by swishing it in cold water in two specially grooved bowls, back and forth from one grooved bowl to the other. There's a real art to the process. Being denser and heavier, rocks in the rice get stuck in the grooves. Once bit by bit all the rocks are painstakingly removed this way, the rice can be given a final wash and then cooked at long last.

Most homes in North Korea still use wood cook stoves. Coal is used for heating, but wood fires are preferred for cooking because the cook can more easily control the temperature of the fire. When cooking rice, the temperature has to be hot enough initially to bring the rice and water to a boil but then reduced to a simmer to allow the rice to cook through without burning. After sifting and washing, a wood fire is made hot and then allowed to burn down to a lower temperature suitable for simmering in a large iron pot.

Breakfasts and dinners are usually large meals, but lunch is lighter to save time. All North Korean meals traditionally consist of rice, soup, kimchi, and a few other vegetarian side dishes. Occasionally, some meat or seafood may provide protein to supplement the usual soybean-based proteins.

In South Korea, soup is typically made by boiling water with miso, a soybean paste, flavored with chili pepper paste or powder. But in North Korea, the miso paste and other soup ingredients are always stir-fried first. This adds more oil, and therefore fat, to the diet. After vegetables like potatoes, squash, or bean curd are fried in oil with seasonings, water is added to bring the soup to a boil.

Most Korean side dishes (in both North and South Korea) require a lot of time and energy to prepare, so these dishes are usually made in large quantities and stored in the fridge. Common side dishes include pickled radishes, kimchi, cucumber, and a variety of root vegetables. North Koreans also often eat a dish that is called "imitation meat". It is a form of bean curd hardened to a meat-like consistency. There are a variety of ways to prepare this imitation meat, but regardless of how it's prepared, it is almost always accompanied by chili pepper seasoning. By the time a person walks home, cooks rice and soup, eats lunch, and then walks back to work, two hours have easily passed.

Work would then resume around 2 p.m. and continue until at least 7 p.m. North Koreans work late. There is no such thing as being paid by the hour in North Korea. Almost all jobs are salaried government positions since the country runs on a socialist system. Our foreign liaison at the hospital confessed to us that he would work late most nights, even as late as 11 p.m.

Once the responsibilities of the day end, people either use public transportation or walk to return home. On the way home, they might stop by a small government-owned produce store or market to pick up groceries for the evening meal. Dinner preparations begin once they arrive home. North Koreans eat dinner late in the evening because they prefer going to bed on a full stomach. Traditionally, the whole family waits for the man of the household to arrive before eating; therefore, families typically eat between nine and eleven at night.

Although the work hours are long, work is not

as fast-paced as it would be in a free market economy. Companies have frequent exercise breaks every day that consist of morning stretch routines or early morning or evening dance routines. Either way, throughout the workday there are times of relaxation, group activities, and opportunities for light exercise.

As foreigners, we would always arrive at the hospital after our local counterparts had already begun work and depart before they ended their workday. We also had a longer weekend. We intentionally took two days off, both Saturday and Sunday, every week. But a North Korean has a one-day weekend with Sunday being their only official day of rest. Even on Sunday, though, they sometimes have community obligations. These obligations may include weeding or pruning the common areas around their apartment complex, planting flowers or trees along neighborhood sidewalks, or practicing for holiday events and community performances.

While we would enjoy a restful day in a park or at a nearby swimming pool on Saturdays, North Koreans would be going through their weekly Saturday ideology training. Throughout the country, every Saturday morning every North Korean meets with a work-specific group to which they are assigned for training on current events, ideology, and self-criticism. The group is selected based on their company or department within the workplace. This certainly serves to unify them in mind and purpose. Trainings are year-round, fifty-two weeks a year.

Little time is left for what we might think of as their personal lives, individual errands, rest, or entertainment. Just about every household in North Korea owns a television, but there are only a few channels to choose from. In recent years, DVD releases of movies and television series have become popular. North Korea produces its own animations but also distributes the most popular Disney and Pixar films in local DVD stores.

Rather than being left to the individual to choose for themselves, entertainment is mostly provided, sometimes as a perk in the workplace. Work groups will get bused to orchestra performances, live band concerts, and picnics. Whenever any free time is available, families will enjoy a vacation. Popular family destinations include amusement parks, swimming pools, mountain hiking, and beaches.

For the most part, work is the priority. When they put their mind to it, North Koreans feel they can accomplish just about anything. This has been true since the founding of their nation. Even without technology, they've accomplished huge feats and created massive structures with manpower alone. This work mentality is referred to as "Chollima Speed", which comes from the Chollima Movement in the late 1950's that emphasized ideological incentives to work harder for the economic development of the country.

An example of Chollima in motion is the Nampo Dam or the West Sea Barrage. In just five years from 1981 to 1986, eight kilometers of seawater were dammed off using dump trucks, dikes, and shovels. The dam was built to prevent seawater from flowing into the fresh water of the Daedong River which was used for irrigation. The dam also allows the passage of ships carrying up to 50,000 tons,[34] and is considered one of North Korea's major accomplishments.

The power of North Korea is her people. Every individual, whether from the upper class or the working class serves his country. Each citizen participates in community service on a regular basis by farming state-owned farms, servicing rural communities, and cleaning their local neighborhood streets. This community service is above and beyond their jobs and family responsibilities.

In the minds of North Koreans, it is their hard

work that has allowed them to stand strong as a nation in the midst of opposition from the rest of the world. The North Korean people see themselves as riders of the Chollima, a mythical flying horse that can travel 1,000 li or 400 km in a single day. Their hard work ethic comes from their will to strive for success and victory over all challenges and opposition.

CHAPTER 8

All for One and One for All

On occasion, we had the opportunity as medical humanitarian workers to visit medical centers and clinics outside of our normal work routine in North Korea. Several times we visited the Maternity Hospital in Pyongyang, a state-of-the-art facility by North Korean standards that was constructed in 1980. It boasts the country's most up-to-date technology for women's health and maternity. More recently in the past few years, a breast cancer ward was newly added to the main hospital. This new ward is built like a hotel with marble floors and chandelier lighting. All women in North Korea have mandatory bi-annual breast exams, the focus being on the young to allow for early cancer detection and prevention.

However, while we were visiting the hospital once, the hospital director made an interesting remark. We asked him what the top medical problem was that he routinely saw in his practice. He explained, "For men, we often see lung cancer and liver problems because of smoking and drinking habits. But women in North Korea do not smoke.

Therefore, our main emphasis is to prevent women-related diseases, such as breast cancer."

As I pondered this question, two aspects of his response stuck in my mind. If men smoke, aren't women exposed to second-hand smoke? And I was completely taken aback by matter-of-fact way he had remarked that women in North Korea do not smoke. How could he declare that so categorically? Do women in North Korea not have the freedom to smoke?

It may be that North Korean women have the legal freedom to smoke, but culturally it is just not acceptable. Even though more and more women in South Korea have taken up smoking in recent generations, traditionally women did not smoke unless they were from a more worldly background. How could this hospital director be so confident in his declaration of fact?

The truth is that the Korean people as a whole, but particularly North Koreans, are one of the most intensely collectivistic cultures on earth. This is demonstrated in their slogans: "One for All and All for One", "One United Heart", and "If the Party Decides It, We Do It". But ultimately this collectivistic mindset comes from ancient roots in their particular Asian culture.

Synchronized performances such as that of

the Arirang Mass Games is another display of collectivistic unity, one for which North Korea has become famous. The show begins with the performance of children sitting together in the bleachers on the back side of the arena. Each holds a book of colored plates. They memorize which color from this book to raise in the air when, on cue. Each becomes like a pixel in a larger picture, the whole forming intricate images behind the main performance, just like a living computer screen. Just to make sure that the audience knows these are live people performing and not some computerized technology, right before the performance, the director of the student performers has them practice a few cues. The students shout out in unison as they switch colors. Once the performance begins and the complex backdrop images are revealed, it is mind-boggling how these students can produce such beautiful, complicated mosaics. The Mass Games is a two-hour long performance, but unlike the other performers, these students have no breaks. They perform from beginning to end the entire length of the show. In all the performances I have seen over the years, I have rarely seen a mistake in the background mosaic.

Of course that is only the backdrop behind the main performances. The foreground performance involves tens of thousands of more people who put on complicated dances, gymnastic routines, taekwondo displays, and parades in absolute unison. Their lines are perfectly straight with arms, legs, elbows, and heads all pointed in the same direction at exactly the same moment.

The Arirang Mass Games is broadcast over the entire nation to ensure that the whole population of North Korea can see this perfect example of many acting as one. Other performances are also broadcast several times a year from the Kim Il-Sung Square in Pyongyang, including military parades and anniversary dances on special occasions and state holidays.

I suspect that there is no other place on earth where collectivistic culture is as strong as it is in North Korea. Loyalty to the group is seen in both North and South. Korean culture is fundamentally a group culture. Koreans from both North and South spend the vast majority of their waking hours serving the particular group to which they belong. It might be their department at work, or their graduating class at school, or their community network. Whatever it is, the group takes precedence even over their family.

Since our family typically lived in North Korea for nine months of the year, this meant that our minders or guides had to be with us that entire time. When tourists come to visit North Korea, their minders simply take rooms in the hotel with them. However, for us, since we were long-term residents, our presence required months of sacrifice from our minders. They could not go home for months at a time.

I often felt terrible about this. Because our family chose not to be separated for months at a time we forced our North Korean minders to be separated from theirs. We tried to alleviate the situation by staying home Sunday afternoons just so that our guide could go home to see his family for that one evening a week at least. Sometimes he went home and sometimes he didn't. Once I pleaded with one of them, "Please go home to see your family! I feel terrible that because our family is here in Pyongyang you have to be separated from your family!"

His response was cool and collected. "Don't worry! It's no problem. It's my job." Although our guides may have had extreme circumstances compared to the typical working North Korean, it is common for all North Korean citizens to have work assignments that take them away from their families from time to time. For them, work and country will always take priority over anything else.

One of the main distinctions between North and South Korea is North Korea's extreme loyalty to the nation and to their people. Common slogans proclaim their passion for their country including "Ethnic Pride" and "Let's Do It Our Way" plastered in large, bold red letters. Above family, above even themselves, North Koreans serve their country.

CHAPTER 9

North Korean Socialism

Once we began building our Spine Rehabilitation Center in Pyongyang and treating children with developmental disabilities, word got out in our circles back home that we were established there and we began to receive a steady stream of visitors. This may sound ridiculous, but that's what happened. A few of those years we ended up hosting visitors nonstop all year long, back to back or within one or two weeks of each other. Most of our guests were from the United States or China, but we also had visitors from the Philippines, Russia, and Japan.

On one such occasion we had a group arriving from Hong Kong. In preparation for the visit, one of them kept asking us the same question over and over again. "Where should I exchange money? How can I obtain North Korean currency?" Our answer never seemed to satisfy him. "Just bring U.S. dollars or Chinese renminbi. Those currencies can be used here." This answer just did not make any sense to him, so he would repeat his question in his next message. It was not until he physically arrived in Pyongyang that he understood what we were trying to say!

We knew what he was thinking. Normally, when arriving in a foreign country, one exchanges money into local currency in order to buy anything in local shops and markets. Food, hotel, transportation, basic necessities, and souvenirs all generally require local currency.

North Korea is an exception to that norm. Local currency, for the most part, is only for locals. Foreigners are not meant to obtain or use it on a regular basis. The only places foreigners use local currency are the Unification Market, a type of flea market or farmer's market in Pyongyang that is open to foreigners,[35] as well as certain select department stores. Most areas foreigners are taken accept only foreign currency. The euro is the currency of choice, followed by the U.S. dollar, and least preferred is Chinese renminbi. All hotels, taxis, foreign-goods stores, and restaurants not only accept foreign currency, they don't accept local currency, and some even request euros only.

The North Korean economy is complicated. It's what is generally described as a controlled economy of course (as opposed to a free market economy). There are at least three separate tiers to it that operate simultaneously. The most basic is the original communist token system, an archaic socialist system harking back to North Korea's mid-century formation that still exists today despite many subsequent economic reforms. The salary all government employees receive is part of this token or ration system. Once they receive their salary, they are able to take it to special governmental stores that exchange the tokens for food items and other necessities at artificially low rates so that the items are practically free. These items are distributed by the government as part of their socialist system. For the most part, in theory at least, a North Korean citizen can just get by on the rations the government provides.

In North Korea all basic necessities are provided by the government. This includes housing, education, medical care, as well as basic food and clothing. These bare necessities are provided essentially free of charge by the state. Individuals may not be able to choose where they live or work but they do not have to worry about paying rent or mortgage.

Unsurprisingly, this is not actually enough for most people to live on. Government-provided housing is in short supply, and young married couples just starting out must often live with their in-laws. No luxury items or nice clothing are provided by the government. Any additional items a person may need beyond bare necessities also have to be purchased outside of the token system.

The second tier of the economy, the actual main economy of ordinary North Koreans, involves their own currency called the "won." One U.S. dollar is worth approximately 8,000 North Korean won. Locally produced products as well as products imported from China are bought and sold at this level of the economy. All local markets and department stores use the local currency as well as shops along the street that sell snacks, flowers, Korean fast food, and drinks.

Foreigners can purchase using local currency in two places. At the Unification Market foreign currency can be exchanged directly for local money. Since it is a market run by local, primarily female entrepreneurs, the market accepts only North Korean currency. This market is where ordinary North Koreans are able to supplement their government-issued salaries by producing items at home to sell or exchange.

The real economic power behind the local currency is the women of the country. As homemakers, they are the ones who make and sell items in the market, on the streets, or even from home, becoming self-made business owners who fuel the livelihoods of all ordinary North Koreans. While North Korean men are preoccupied in governmental jobs, it is the women who are the workforce of the marketplace. Older, married women garden at home or make home-made products to sell in the local farmer's market. Younger, unmarried women make up the workforce of the factories in North Korea. As women work in the marketplace or at local factories, they improve the lives of their family members.

The second place foreigners can purchase with local currency are the specially designated department stores where they can exchange money at exchange booths and where they can also purchase local cash cards. Money from any accepted currency can be deposited directly to a cash card which can then be used as a debit card. Cash cards are now widely used in North Korea. Some department stores use only their own specific cash card, but in general, a Koryo cash card can be obtained at the Koryo Hotel[36] or other hotels.

The Koryo cash card is strictly for foreign currency users. There are advantages to using it as a foreign visitor. For one, they are extremely convenient and can be used at foreign-goods grocery stores, gas stations, hotels, and even at local restaurants. Since three different currencies are accepted in North Korea in addition to the won, it can be difficult to get correct change back. Sometimes you will get euros for change instead of U.S. dollars. At other times, it will be Chinese renminbi. If the store or restaurant really does not have any foreign currency available, you might even get items like gum or a drink back for your change instead of cash. Using cash cards can help you save money by eliminating the need for change.

So foreign visitors to North Korea really do have no immediate need for local currency. Hotels, restaurants, and stores approved for foreigners all accept foreign currency. But mind you, they only accept crisp new bills. A wrinkled or torn bill will be rejected.

What we found while living there is that North Koreans are eager to improve their economy and venture into the international market. Koreans, whether from the North or the South, are cunning businessmen, an inherent trait that exists in North Korea still despite years of a controlled economy and limited economic opportunity.

The government, of course, employs just about everyone and also owns the land and the businesses. Apart from farmers' markets and home-made products, it is generally not possible for a North Korean to own a major business or company. The one exception is the food industry. Some local people do own restaurants and coffee shops, but by and large, all businesses in North Korea are government-run. Almost all land and property are owned by the government, including state farms. Therefore, food supply and production are primarily a government responsibility.

Aside from times of nation-wide shortages which occurred most famously in the late 1990's, citizens in the city have access to basic needs. When international news media describe North Korea as a starving, impoverished nation journalists are often quoting outdated information. North Koreans do not need to worry about housing, basic food and clothing, or education and health care. All these things are available to them free of charge, at least they are so long as families can afford to pay the expected tip for the services. In large cities, public transportation is also provided. Individuals are not allowed to own personal vehicles, so any vehicle on the road is either a company car or a foreign-owned vehicle. In general, problems only arise when material resources are unavailable.

North Koreans find it hard to grasp the concept of for-profit business. They are intuitively aware of general business concepts, but without the experience, cannot truly identify with the sacrifice required to invest in and grow a business in hopes of substantial profit.

In Rason and other special economic zones where the North Korean government has been experimenting with foreign investment, several small foreign businesses came in with moderate success. The few largescale investments that attempted to launch failed because of the high threshold cost of doing business in North Korea. The only foreign businesses still operating in the special economic zones are social enterprises that are businesses in theory but consist more of not-for-profit humanitarian operations running at cost and generating little income.

What makes investment in North Korea so expensive is the fact that all property is owned by the state and the state can and does arbitrarily increase costs for foreigners at whim. This not only makes operation costs extremely high but also unpredictable. In addition, labor is not as cheap as one might expect. Other third-world countries are more cost-effective because North Korea requires foreign businesses to pay exorbitant income taxes for local employees. On top of all this, since the entire country is a government-operated socialist system, officials expect "favors" as part of regular business practices.

Since the basic economy runs on so little currency, favors are a means to give and receive what is needed. Therefore, doing business requires an exchange in favors or gifts.

For example, the average North Korean doctor is paid a salary of less than one U.S. dollar a week. No one can actually thrive on that income, yet doctors are highly educated and respected in North Korea, as they are everywhere in the world. Although the health care system is free of charge, it is understood that a patient should bring a "Thank You" gift or tip to the doctor each time he or she is treated. This ensures that the doctor has an income he or she can live on as well as enabling the doctor to maintain the respectable status of a physician. If the gifts given the doctor are items that are not needed by the doctor's family, then they can be exchanged or sold at the local farmer's market. These gifts can also be used to barter with in exchange for plumbing or electrical work or some other needed service or favor from someone else.

Foreigners working and living in North Korea are usually expected to give at least the standard gift or favor, but unfortunately, are almost never the recipients of any such gifts. Always giving and never receiving in this locally understood economic system causes the cost of business to become too great for most.

Currently, although possible, it is very challenging to make an above board for-profit business successful in North Korea, particularly if it is a foreign-owned business. Without the U.N. sanctions, doing business in North Korea would be challenging. But with the sanctions preventing North Korean goods from being exported, it is all but impossible. The internal buying power of North Korea is increasing, but without the input of foreign currency in this third global tier of the economy, it is not likely to grow much further.

If North Korea were able to operate freely in international markets, they could potentially thrive in business. But, it will take individuals time for them to acclimate to the international market, including standard business practices, and for them to switch from their socialist mindsets to doing business in a capitalistic world. For now, North Korea continues to function on a dual system.

봉수교회

CHAPTER 10

Religion in an Atheistic Nation

North Korea may not have freedom of religion to the extent that America does, but there is a limited degree of religious tolerance. In recent years, I have experienced positive changes in regards to the expression and practice of religion in North Korea.

Our family had the privilege of living in close proximity to one of the official protestant churches in Pyongyang. This gave us the opportunity of walking to church on Sunday. Every Sunday morning, we took a brisk 30 to 40-minute walk to the near-by church. We came to know and greet the same people week after week, and we were able to experience a glimpse of normal life as we walked through local neighborhoods on our way to church. After church, the local parishioners would sometimes stop to say a few words, politely greet us, and give us a warm wave good-bye as their smiles gave color to the drabness of gray surroundings.

As a Communist nation, North Korea is officially atheist. Instead of looking to faith or religion, they seek answers in material humanism, namely in what human effort can produce, especially collectively when masses of people unite for a single purpose. This is the basis of Juche, their peculiar national philosophy.

North Korea's aversion to religion is rooted in their past. They experienced the use of religion to oppress and control a citizenry first hand during the Japanese occupation. Koreans were forced to bow to Japanese Shinto shrines and if they refused, they were imprisoned and sometimes even killed. This forced worship at Shinto shrines was not just about religion. It was also about nationalism and cultural identity. Koreans were not only forced to submit to Japanese administrative rule but also to Japanese culture, religion, and even language. Korean was outlawed during the occupation, and all Koreans were forced to learn and speak Japanese. Religion was just one aspect of this oppression. After the occupation, North Korea joined other communist nations in condemning religion as a means of political control. From their own experiences with religious oppression they at first decided they wanted no more part of any form of religion at all.

When the Communists took control of North Korea in 1948, the new government began persecuting Christians. Churches were closed and

North Korean Christians were subjected to intense pressure to stop practicing their faith. Those who refused were labeled rebels against the regime.

During the Korean War, most Christians in North Korea fled south. Very few remained by the end of the war. Since their enemy the U.S. was portrayed as a Christian nation, North Koreans harbored deep resentment towards Christians. Unlike in South Korea, North Koreans labeled Christianity a Western religion used to control people and outlawed it. Any Christians left in North Korea were forced underground.

North Korea's pre-communist religious roots are similar to those of the South. Shamanism, Buddhism, and Confucianism have been the religious cornerstones of Korean culture for thousands of years. Shamanism is the original folk religion of Korea; whereas Buddhism and Confucianism were the result of Chinese influence. Christianity was introduced later as well but is the only religion in North Korea considered a strictly foreign religion.

Associating Christianity with American imperialism, North Koreans are taught in school that Christian missionaries in the eighteen and nineteen hundreds only came to Korea to indoctrinate people with Western civilization. During the Korean War, they are taught, U.S. soldiers massacred

Koreans like modern day crusaders. The fact that it was Korean Christians who were the largest group that opposed communism when it took over the government in 1948 is something that only fans the flames of hatred for Christianity on the part of the establishment. In North Korea, Christians are considered spies, foreign imperialists, and anti-government traitors.

Despite these official anti-religious sentiments, most North Koreans still do follow traditional shamanistic practices. They believe in good and bad luck, they follow superstitions and use charms to ward off evil or attract good. People in the countryside rely on shamanistic remedies to cure ailments. Additionally, North Koreans are followers of Confucius since so much of the culture is rooted in Confucianism. The main remnant of religious Confucianism still practiced today is ancestor worship. Every year on Chusok, Korea's Fall Harvest Festival, families gather to pay reverent respects to their deceased loved ones.

It might seem ironic or incongruous that in their constitution North Koreans have freedom of religion. However, this isn't the freedom for individuals to choose their religion, it is the freedom for those with religious roots to continue honoring their history. For example, Buddhism is still active in North Korea to a minimal degree. North Korea preserved their Buddhist temples mainly for historical purposes and at each, North Korean Buddhist monks continue to serve and maintain the religious practices of the temple.

Similarly, Christianity is now allowed to persist in North Korea even though the vast majority of churches were destroyed during the early years of communism. In 1989, Kim Il-Sung rebuilt the home church of his mother and thus gave new life to the practice of Christianity in North Korea. It turns out that Kim Il-Sung's own mother was a Christian, which fact led him to restore the church near her family home in the Chil-Gol District of Pyongyang. Since then, two other state churches were built, one Protestant church and one Catholic church.

Living in North Korea we sometimes felt as though we had reached the limits of what foreigners could learn about the nation. But then, someone or something would surprise us.

In the summer of 2013, we hosted the first foreign visitors to our home in Pyongyang. This couple were friends of the family, supporters of our work in the country who shared our Christian faith. As we were to do with so many others, we gave them a tour of some of the sites. One day this couple was riding in the car with us while one of our guides was explaining the history of the city, providing us with random, touristy type facts. In the middle of the tour, he suddenly blurted out, "Pyongyang is the birthplace of Christianity in Korea. It was once known as the Jerusalem of the East." We knew he was referring to the 1907 great revival in Pyongyang, but we were shocked! Was this official North Korean guide actually admitting to us that Christianity in Korea and perhaps more of the East began in Pyongyang?

Foreigners in North Korea have the freedom to worship in our own way in our own home. There is a Muslim mosque in Pyongyang for employees of Muslim embassies in Pyongyang, and there is a Russian Orthodox Church for the Russian embassy employees. So far, no Protestant or Catholic Church has been established specifically for foreigners, but foreigners are allowed to attend services at officially recognized state churches.

By the time we had lived in Pyongyang for about five years, we were attending one of these state churches regularly. These churches have been ridiculed by foreigners as being mere "facades."[37] Foreigners think that the congregations just go through the motions of worship because they are ordered to do so by the government, not because they choose to believe. The churches have also been ridiculed as a mere facade of religious freedom in North Korea.[38] It is true that religious freedom does not exist for the vast majority of North Koreans. It is also true that religious freedom is nominally part of the 1949 North Korean constitution and show-cased by these churches.

After having attended these churches ourselves week in and week out for some years, we are convinced that there is a degree of genuine faith among the members. From what we understand, many of the church-goers have a Christian heritage. In the services, members of the congregation typically do not show much expression unless they are up front performing during worship. But every once in a while, you might see a church member silently singing along with the choir, reading Scripture, or praying reverently.

Since we attended the same church on such a regular basis, we came to know the pastor and his staff well. Speaking with the pastor gave us even more insight into how Christianity is officially recognized in North Korea. According to the pastor, in addition to the two Protestant state churches and one Catholic state church, there are around twenty officially registered house churches in Pyongyang. The North Korean Protestant seminary is even located just behind one of the Protestant state churches. It trains and graduates a class of new pastors whenever there is a demand for pastors. The last class included ten seminary students. Once these students graduate, they are commissioned to go serve the government recognized house churches. Seminary training lasts approximately two years, and although there are not many resources available for the seminary students, in recent years, foreigners have been allowed to donate religious books to the seminary.

The highlight of attending the state churches is meeting other Christian foreigners in North Korea. Not everyone has time in their schedule to visit church on Sunday, but many do make an effort to attend services. At the end of the service, the pastor invites the foreign guests to share a word of encouragement or a special song, if they like. For us, the best part of the service was when tour groups came and performed special songs for the congregation.

One time a tour group consisting of fifty-four different nationalities visited our church. They called themselves "Rainbow Tourism" as they represented a mosaic of races and cultures from around the world. The guests arrived in three tour buses with 150 people. Needless to say, it was a rare sight in Pyongyang! The guests that day far out-numbered the local congregation. When the pastor invited the group to share at the end of the service, the group's leader stood up and read Isaiah 63, proclaiming it over the congregation and the nation. Then, the entire group gathered at the front of the church to sing "Amazing Grace".

The most surprising part of it was when at the end of the service, as the members of the congregation were leaving to head home, the tourists once again gathered to sing "Amazing Grace," this time outside on the steps of the chapel! The song floated through the air and could be heard throughout the entire neighborhood. As the main group sang, others waved banners in front of the steps, and the leader of the group narrated for the camera as they documented the occasion.

North Korea is infamous for its lack of religious freedom. But there is a new spirit of religious freedom entering the land. Right now, this freedom is primarily for foreigners living in North Korea, but I hope and believe it is the start of something new. In this atheist land, a crack is beginning to form, broadening tolerance and understanding for people with different cultures, views, and faiths.

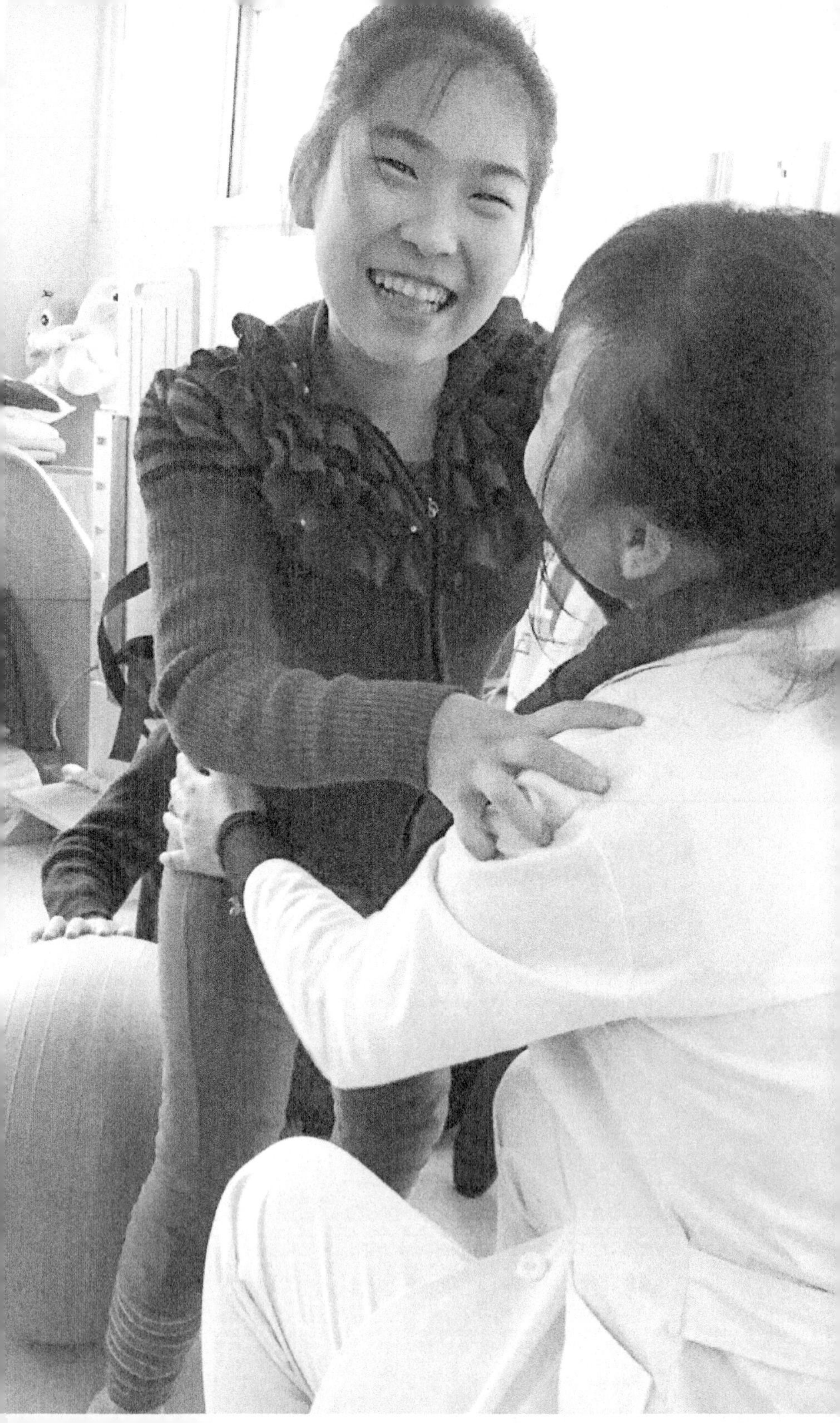

CHAPTER 11

Free Healthcare

Blessing was the daughter of an official we met in the economic zone. Like most disabled children in North Korea, Blessing was kept secretly at home. The official's closest friends did not even know that his daughter existed. At the age of four, she could not walk, stand, or even sit-up. Blessing was quadriplegic.

Blessing came from her province several days' journey away to be treated at our hospital. She was one of the first pediatric patients of her kind to be admitted to the hospital in Pyongyang. Not only were the parents of the other pediatric patients surprised to see a quadriplegic child being treated in the hospital, but the other doctors and staff in the hospital were equally shocked. As they observed Blessing getting a little better each day, they began to think of other children who were hidden away in their own villages and towns whom they knew. Soon the parents in Blessing's in-patient room started to call friends and family back home. Not even a month went by before mothers and their disabled children began to line up outside the hospital for treatment.

Blessing's story is just one example of North Korea's health system. Along with housing and education, healthcare is considered free in North Korea. There is no co-pay to patients for doctor visits, no patient bills for examinations or lab tests. Even surgery is fully covered. Medication is available for a minimal charge, and healthcare is accessible to all citizens throughout the country.

In the countryside, villages have small clinics called *Ri* clinics that serve the local people. Morning hours are reserved for outpatient appointments, and in the afternoon doctors conduct house visits. If the *Ri* clinic cannot provide adequate care, the case is referred to a clinic in the city. A city clinic may be several miles or kilometers away, so to get there patients might catch a ride on a local truck heading that direction or possibly pay to ride the city-to-city bus, if one is available.

City hospitals are better equipped with surgical centers and other medical departments. *Ri* clinics are strictly just country clinics, run by family and general practitioners who cover all medical needs including obstetrics and gynecology. If a city hospital cannot provide the needed expertise, the case is referred to a provincial hospital. There are eleven provinces in North Korea with Pyongyang City being designated as its own provincial district. The most difficult cases are referred to the tertiary hospital in Pyongyang.

In comparison to the rest of the country, Pyongyang is more highly developed in terms of modern medical practices and standards. In the past ten years or so, the government has built new hospitals and medical centers for Pediatrics, Breast Cancer, and Ophthalmology. The fact remains that there is still a large gap between standards of care in North Korea and in the West. Even though North Korean doctors are often able to receive some education from abroad, medical supplies and equipment in North Korea are outdated. Not only is up-to-date equipment not available in most cases but neither are reliable power sources to run them.

One reason for the lag is that North Korea requires doctors studying abroad to be fully funded by the host nations, not just for the cost of tuition but also for room and board. Few such programs are available. Another reason given is that the country is still in a war-time mentality. The military receives priority when it comes to medical care because the state is focused on ensuring that all able-bodied persons are fit to contribute to the preservation of the country. Physicians are primarily tasked with remedying acute diseases. To put all of this in perspective, however, the most common medical issue for children is diarrhea, a problem that might be described as rampant.

Several pressing medical issues are very concerning in North Korea. Perhaps the most concerning is wide-spread tuberculosis. Not only is tuberculosis common in North Korea, but the antibiotic-resistant strain is also prevalent. Therefore, in order to treat this contagious and life-threatening disease, expensive medication is needed that unfortunately, is often too expensive for humanitarian workers to provide and is not generally available.

One of our biggest challenges as medical humanitarian workers in North Korea was the lack of emphasis there on medical needs beyond the scope of immediate, acute diseases. Most North Korean medical care is focused on contagious diseases such as tuberculosis, hepatitis, and diarrhea. Although support from international organizations has helped improve treatment, the mindset of North Koreans has been slow to modernize.

For example, the largest maternity hospital in Pyongyang, is overly concerned with the prevention of contagious diseases. In Western nations, mothers are united with their babies soon or immediately after giving birth for skin-to-skin contact, which research has demonstrated is vital to bonding, which in turn is important for neonatal development. Even if hospitals restrict visitors, immediate family members are able to stay in the hospital with mother and baby. In countries like the United States, fathers are even welcome in the delivery room to witness their child's entry into the world.

In Pyongyang, in what is considered the best maternity hospital in the country, mothers are separated from both baby and family. Instead of being handed to the new mom at birth, newborns are immediately taken straight to the nursery by the nursing staff. Fathers and other immediate family members are not allowed in and can only talk to the mother via video conferencing. Mothers are quarantined to prevent the threat of disease. Only at a mother's request is she eventually able to hold her baby at least a day or more after the birth. Disease prevention takes precedence over maternal bonding.

It was challenging for us as foreign humanitarian workers to work in a medical system so focused on contagious diseases and acute care issues. Many long-term medical issues in North Korea are simply being left unresolved in the shadows.

With our combined educations, Stephen and I were uniquely well-suited to work with children with disabilities. We are humbled by what we were able to accomplish in the time that we were there. Through our project and those of a few other organizations, treatment for children with developmental disabilities is now available for the first time in North Korea. Before we came to Pyongyang, there was no medical training or therapy to treat children with developmental disabilities like cerebral palsy or autism. Both conditions were considered untreatable due to a lack of expertise.

Now North Korea is implementing treatment and education for children with developmental disabilities in the medical university system for the first time thanks to new training programs in Rehabilitation Medicine and Special Education. Initially, the local hospital administrator did not acknowledge the existence of developmental disabilities, such as cerebral palsy and autism, in the nation. But as patients came to be treated in the hospital, the need to treat pediatric developmental disabilities was officially recognized.

In the fall of 2013, a ten-year-old girl came to us diagnosed with spastic quadriplegia, a type of cerebral palsy that affects both arms and legs. Her life up to that point had been one of heartbreaking challenges. She couldn't walk so her classroom teacher would strap her to her back and carry her to school every morning. At school her teacher would then strap her to her chair for her to remain seated and listen to the class lectures. This girl's greatest dream at that time was simply to walk to school one day with the rest of her classmates. Once treatment for children with cerebral palsy began officially in 2013, she was finally able to receive medical care through the system.

She came to us, and after approximately eleven months of daily therapy, she realized her dream. She walked out of the hospital! A local news network broadcast team came and televised her discharge from the hospital. Today she is attending school with the rest of her classmates and has a new dream. Her dream is to become a rehab physician so that she can treat other kids like herself.

Thousands of children like her are waiting for medical treatment in North Korea. Many of them have never attended school but through our therapy program for children with developmental disabilities, these children now have hope for a better future.

Seeing the positive impact of the Pyongyang hospital's successful treatment of children with cerebral palsy, the North Korean Department of Public Health is now working to establish Pediatric Rehabilitation Centers in all ten provincial hospitals. Doctors are also being trained in treatment methodologies at Kim Il-Sung University Pyongyang Medical School Hospital. The government has ensured the development of this specialty in all 10 medical schools in the country by signing an agreement with our sponsoring organization. Even the former Leader Kim Jong-Il, and current Leader Kim Jong-Un, signed off on the project!

After partnering with another American therapist in June 2015, the program expanded to include children with Autism Spectrum Disorder (ASD). There had been no diagnosis or therapy of any kind available for children with ASD in the DPRK. It was essentially unknown and both children with ASD and their parents struggled with neither the resources nor skills to cope with the challenges that faced them.

A seven-year-old autistic boy was one of our first patients for this new program for children with ASD. Initially, his eyes were wide with fear. He had never uttered a word before, and as a result had never attended school. He could not tolerate anyone near him and had challenges with sensory processing as well as social communication.

At first he appeared disinterested in the therapist. All he did was sit in a corner spinning a toy to help relieve his anxiety. But then the therapist was able to make eye contact. This child craved physical stimulation, and the therapist found that tickling him opened the doors to his social communication. At the end of a 30-minute session, he was engaged in back-and-forth interaction with the therapist. Laughing loudly, he would grab the therapist's hands and place them on his stomach asking, "More! Tickle me more!" With tears welling in her eyes, his mom exclaimed that he was the happiest she had ever seen him.

In two short years, the Pyongyang Medical School Hospital has made great strides in learning about ASD and available therapies. In cooperation with the Ministry of Public Health, the hospital has hosted a series of four separate weeks of lectures and hands-on therapy skills training provided by humanitarian volunteers. Doctors who have participated in this training will be the pioneers of ASD therapy throughout the nation. In addition to specific skills and techniques to facilitate social interaction and communication in children with ASD, the training included foundational theories and philosophies of practice. Attitudes and perspectives of both doctors and families have changed through the discussions about different models of disability, about holistic child development and about the importance of cultivating trusting relationships with children and families.

Pyongyang Medical School Hospital has recognized the value of this training series and invited others to join them. Over thirty doctors from Pyongyang Medical School Hospital, Pyongyang Children's Hospital, and the DPRK Disability Federation have already taken part. The Assistant Director and Chair of the Neurology Department at Munsoon Rehabilitation Center also expressed interest in participating in future training.

The training on ASD was not only helpful for direct care providers, but also caught the attention of officials from The Ministry of Science and Technology and the Ministry of Public Health. Their increased awareness and education about ASD is crucial in the adaptation of the medical system and formation of policies to include the diagnosis and care for children with ASD and other developmental disabilities.

Children with cerebral palsy, autism, and other developmental disabilities are being helped and starting to participate in their communities thanks to training of medical students in rehabilitation specialties, empowering parents, and igniting change in the society's perspective of disability. One child, family, doctor, and facility at a time, we are seeing our vision become reality.

CHAPTER 12

Learning DPRK Style

One of the privileges we enjoyed living in North Korea was sending our children to school in Pyongyang. For the first several years, we primarily homeschooled our children. In Rason, there were no other options, but when we moved to Pyongyang we were given the opportunity to send our kids to the Pyongyang Korean School for Foreigners. After years of having mom for a teacher and their siblings for classmates, our children were more than happy to go to school with other kids their age.

Located in the Munsu Dong Foreign Embassy Compound on the east side of the city, Pyongyang Korean School for Foreigners educates the children of staff from diplomatic and humanitarian agencies. Although the school is K through 12, there are usually no more than fifty students, but they come from about twenty-five different nations. The community is small but highly diverse because of the numerous embassies and agencies on the foreign compound. Each country is represented at the school by one or two families.

Our children learned and played with kids from Nigeria, Ethiopia, China, Vietnam, Indonesia, Cambodia, Mongolia, Sweden, and more. It was the best cross-cultural education one could find in North Korea. The school focused on math and sciences, and since the children were from all over the world, English was taught as a second language for foreign language learners. Korean, art, music, and physical education were also taught, but no ideology or history. The only social science taught in the school was geography. Our children thoroughly enjoyed going to school in the morning and then supplementing their education through homeschool in the afternoon. Combining the two was demanding. Our children had to keep up with both American and Korean education systems simultaneously, which required them to study practically all day, every day.

Pyongyang Korean School for Foreigners was a unique experience because all the teachers and administrators were North Korean. They would use North Korean textbooks translated into English which made it like attending school in North Korea in English without the classes in ideology. This gave us a glimpse into the education system of North Korea.

As humanitarian workers, we supported

daycare centers, kindergartens, and orphanages throughout North Korea. Each time we visited a kindergarten or school, the children performed for us. Children as young as five or six performed songs and dances to near robotic perfection. Their facial expressions are trained along with the tiniest detail of movement all the way to the twitch of their fingers.

While I struggled as a parent of three to control my own children, North Korean children seem perfectly well-behaved. It is only after the performance, when they go out in the playground or the school yard that their individual personalities and playfulness come out.

Every semester, the Pyongyang Korean School for Foreigners has a sports day and takes a field trip, including a picnic outing. When our youngest daughter was in kindergarten, I often went with her on school field trips. We would go hiking at a local mountain or enjoy the nearby amusement park, zoo, or botanical gardens. On one of these field trips, we visited the Children's Palace in Pyongyang. This was my second or third time visiting this elaborate training center for children's extra-curricular activities. Children in Pyongyang who wish can go to the Children's Palace to learn anything from music and dance to sports and art.

Several hours every afternoon is dedicated to an extra-curricular activity of choice. Once a choice is made, the children have the opportunity to excel in their activity.

On this particular visit, it dawned on me how North Korean children could be so well-behaved, and likewise, what was expected of our children from their North Korean teachers. During our one-hour visit at the Children's Palace, we toured room after room of children participating in their extra-curricular activities. We were never able to stay in one room more than five to ten minutes at a time because there were so many rooms to visit. Whole performances could only be seen in the main auditorium when the palace put on an official show.

In each room we visited, the instructor's teaching style was similar. Several seconds of practice would go by, and then the teacher would stop and correct the students. The teacher was constantly finding imperfections in the students' performances, imperfections I was never able to discern myself. They would practice the same thing over and over again until they reached complete perfection.

For the most part, our children thoroughly enjoyed attending school in North Korea. The teachers were kind and warm-hearted, doing their best to serve a group of students from diverse backgrounds. The teachers at Pyongyang Korean School for Foreigners are the very cream of the crop of teachers. They speak fluent English and are experts in their fields. Most of all, it was an amazing opportunity for our children to befriend kids from other places around the world whom they otherwise would never have met.

Of course, there were a few struggles adjusting to another culture and to the way that they do school. Since our lives were so mobile and we traveled often, there were times we had to miss a substantial amount of school. We were grateful for the school's understanding of our nomadic lifestyle and for the way they accommodated our family's schedule. But it was difficult for our kids to keep up with school while we were away. This was more than the normal struggles of homeschooling. Textbooks in North Korea are written so that in order to properly learn a subject, the student must learn directly from the teacher. Teachers fill in information gaps that are not covered in the textbook. Curriculum is developed so as to ensure that the student is dependent on the teacher. In North Korea pupils are not meant to learn in isolation.

Our children also struggled with the intense

drive for perfection in North Korea. No matter how well they did, their teachers expected more. Nothing short of a perfect score would do!

In our work with children with disabilities, we found this to be a particular challenge. Children with disabilities will never be "perfect" in the sense that they will always have some remnant of their disability. In an individualistic culture, it is easier on differences, but in a collectivistic culture, everyone is expected to conform to the social norm.

Every year our organization was invited to the DPRK Handicap Association performance. This is a time designated to celebrate the advancements North Korea is making for people with disabilities. Most of the achievements have been for those with sight-impairments, hearing-impairments, as well as a few physical impairments. Currently, there are schools for the blind and schools for the deaf in North Korea. A recently built Rehabilitation Center in Pyongyang is also serving children with various other disabilities. Every year these children put on a performance celebrating their collective achievements.

In 2016, the event surpassed all expectations. All the children who performed had some form of disability, but most of them were either hearing-impaired or sight-impaired. They presented dances, music, and even magic acts. Their performances were nothing short of perfection. It was absolutely astonishing.

I left the performance with a lot of questions though. What did this mean for our work with children with developmental disabilities if even children with disabilities in North Korea are expected to be perfect? And how should I better supplement my education at home for our children in light of what I was learning about the North Korean education system? Most importantly, what did this say about how the average North Korean feels they must behave and who they must become?

Many of these questions remain unanswered for me. But I did walk away from that performance with a new perspective. Expectations placed on North Koreans are extremely high. Despite obstacles in their path, each person is expected to overcome their difficulties to achieve success. Above all, people are expected to reach or even surpass social expectations. This is central to North Korea's education. As their slogan states, "Learn for the Country!"

CHAPTER 13

Korean Dynasties

Living and working overseas, it was easy to get to know people from around the world, people who like us had left their own nations to follow a calling or profession in North Korea. We called this group our expat community. It was not just expatriates from the United States but also Sweden, Germany, Canada, Switzerland, the Netherlands, Australia, and others.

One of our friends in the expat community in Pyongyang was from Poland. He was interested in the North Korea outside the capital city and so with this curiosity decided to take a trip to explore the countryside. At the end of his trip, I asked him what he thought about North Korea. I was particularly interested to hear what he had to say coming from a former communist nation himself. This is what he concluded, "In Poland, we always viewed communism as something imposed on us by a foreign power (Russia), but in North Korea I discovered that communism is a nationalistic movement, of the people and for the people. The people really believe in it."

He was right. Communism in North Korea is viewed as deliverance from Japanese Imperialism. Comrade Kim Il-Sung was the morning star that saved them from the tyranny of Japanese control. After leading the fight for independence, General Kim Il-Sung returned from his military base in China to establish a government for the Korean people in 1948. A revolutionary leader in the fight for independence from the Japanese and born into humble circumstances, he was one of them! He was their hero.

In North Korean lore about the Founding Leader, General Kim Il-Sung was known for spending time with the people on their level. He would go to the countryside and sit on straw mats and discuss issues with local farmers. He would personally oversee every tiny detail in the development of his country. At the end of the Korean War, he motivated his people to rebuild their country from the rubble and ashes.

North Koreans have always had a special place in their hearts for their founding leader. He touched many of their families in personal ways. We once heard an account of how one particular family was blessed by the generosity and benevolence of General Kim Il-Sung. It took all night to patiently listen to all the many, many details of the ways he blessed them! When General Kim Il-Sung died in 1994, the entire country was seen weeping and crying out in mourning. Many have questioned whether or not those tears were genuine. We think they were.

North Korea has an unusually large number of holidays. These are not like Thanksgiving or Christmas for Americans, meant for spending time with family and friends and getting a break from one's job. North Korean holidays celebrate the state's political accomplishments and milestones. It seems like there is a separate holiday for the founding day of each bureau within the government.

For the more significant holidays, there are national events that people either participate in or attend. This is to maintain and spur on national loyalty. Usually these events occur in governmental buildings or town squares.

For the 100th birthday of Kim Il-Sung, our family had the privilege of attending the celebrations at Kim Il-Sung Square. The leader of the country rarely leaves the security of his palace, but on this occasion, to commemorate the 100th birthday of his grandfather, Chairman Kim Jong-Un gave a speech at the square.

His voice was nothing spectacular, but as he

spoke, a few older women near me began to weep. They were overcome with emotion. Just hearing the voice of the grandson of the Great Leader overwhelmed them as they remembered the father of their nation.

After both General Kim Il-Sung and Chairman Kim Jong-Il's deaths, they were each embalmed and placed in the mausoleum at the Kumsusan Memorial Palace. Their bodies are covered with the North Korean flag. Only their torsos and heads were uncovered for viewing. Several times a year, hundreds of thousands of North Koreans and foreigners solemnly view the bodies and pay their respects to these great and dear highly revered leaders.

People all over the world criticize North Korea's leaders. The news media quote defectors that have had horrific experiences and label North Korea's leaders cruel. A well-rounded picture of North Korea however includes not only these heart-breakingly tragic accounts but also the perspectives of the citizens who remain fully devoted to their leaders and their nation.

A complete picture of North Korea as to include both the good and the bad things that the leaders have done for their nation. We may think that the negative outweighs the good, but in a socialist system, all local people directly receive benefits from their leaders. For example, Chairman Kim Jong-Un, in addition to constructing new apartment complexes in Pyongyang, has undertaken a project to rebuild the orphanages throughout the entire nation. I have visited a number of these renovated orphanages in Pyeongseong and Wonsan myself, and they looked very impressive. The facilities include gymnasiums, swimming pools, playgrounds, as well as nicely-furnished educational, medical, and housing facilities. They are far better than what would normally be provided by a humanitarian organization.

For thousands of years, Korea was ruled by monarchies. Korea had twelve major dynasties, the last being the Joseon Dynasty. From the North Korean perspective, they are simply carrying on in the long legacy of past Korean dynasties. They have no experience of anything else; they know nothing different.

3대헌장

CHAPTER 14

Unification

North Korea has a strong drive for reunification. This is a soft spot for all Koreans, but particularly North Koreans. A regular part of our work was bringing in donors and sponsors of projects to witness first-hand the effect our humanitarian work was having on the common people of North Korea. On one particular trip, we brought in several guests consisting of supporters for our kindergartens in the special economic zone. Because of this special visit, one of the childcare centers we supported decided to perform for our guests. The children and the teachers took turns singing, and then it was our turn!

Towards the end of our time together, we gathered in a circle, holding hands, singing songs of unification and sentimentality. Many tears fell. To my surprise, most of those tears were not just ours but the teachers'. In this schoolroom were Koreans from the North, as well as Koreans formerly from the South, from the U.S., and from Uzbekistan. And then there was me, Joy, a non-Korean privileged to take part in this special Korean bonding time.

When I saw the expression on the faces of the teachers and their tears, my eyes, too, started watering! Working in unity makes a huge difference in North Korea.

Similar to this experience, North Koreans' emotional desire for unification is exemplified in the Arch of Reunification. This is a symbolic sculptural monument that forms a large archway, facing the southern highway heading towards the Demilitarized Zone (DMZ). Officially known as the Three-Point Charter for National Reunification, the arch consists of twin women holding a map of a unified Korea. The women are identical in stature and construction. They represent the two sister nations of Korea, South and North. The monument was opened in 2001 to commemorate Korean unification as put forward by Kim Il-Sung, which consists of Three Principles for National Reunification.[39]

Since that first visit, our family revisited the Arch of Reunification a few times. It is a favorite spot for guests when they visit for the first time. What I personally like most about the monument is that it demonstrates North Korea's passion to unify the Korean nation. North Korea's passion for unification however is not as equally shared by South Korea. No such monument exists there.

Growing up in South Korea, what I heard about North Korea was by and large negative. I grew up during turbulent years in South Korea when mass demonstrations were happening, including the Gwangju Uprising in 1980. Students of Chonnam University and citizens of Gwangju city took up arms to protest the military coup that overtook the nation and established President Chun Doo-Hwan as the new leader of the country. The new president had not yet officially taken office when the Gwangju uprising occurred on May 18, 1980. The government massacred an estimated 606 individuals that day and claimed that the uprising was a rebellion of Communist Sympathizers.[40] This produced strong anti-communist sentiments and fear of communism throughout South Korea. Any individual sympathetic to the communists was placed under surveillance and subjected to torture and in some cases even death.[41]

Negative sentiments towards North Korea enabled South Korea to maintain political strength in uncertain times. The memory of the Korean War was also still vivid in the minds of South Koreans. They not only did not want communist sympathizers in their country but also did not want North Korea to attack again.

For a while, South Korea practiced air sirens

once a month. These drills would last about an hour. When the air siren sounded, people were ordered to go into their homes and pull their curtains shut. Cars on the road had to pull to the curb and wait until the second siren indicated that the drill had ended. Vehicles were all equipped with emergency supplies in the event that war broke out, and all foreigners were asked to register with their local embassies in the event of an evacuation.

This is what I knew of North Korea growing up. The depiction of North Koreans in South Korean textbooks painted a dark picture. South Korean policy of the time decided to promote North Korea-phobia. South Korean textbooks depicted North Koreans as red devils with horns and tails ready to devour the children of the South. It instilled instant fear into the hearts and minds of South Korean children.[42]

Today the people of South Korea are divided. Conservatives do not want to engage with North Korea, but liberals are willing to open up and discuss unification. Each president that comes into office in South Korea has a different policy towards the North, and since presidents are elected every five years in South Korea with the ability to serve only one term, there is no long-term policy towards North Korea.

South Korea does have a Ministry of Unification within the government established to promote Korean reunification. There are several bureaus under the Ministry of Unification, offices for inter-Korean dialogue, bureaus for unification policy, humanitarian cooperation, and inter-Korean exchanges and consultation.[43] Of course, the Ministry of Unification's policy direction also changes whenever a new South Korean president is elected. Overall, South Korea is less enthusiastic about reunification because they assume that the economic rehabilitation of North Korea would become their primary financial burden, as it became for West Germany after German reunification.

North Korea on the other hand has remained consistently enthusiastic about reunification. Every North Korean citizen that I have met expresses strong sentiments for unification with South Korea. Songs such as "Ban Gap Sim Nee Da," translated as "Nice to Meet You" and "Da Shee Man Na Yo" or "Let's Meet Again" emphasize North Korea's heart towards their Korean brothers and sisters throughout the world, including South Korea. More obvious songs, such as the song entitled "Unification", are also sung on a regular basis in North Korea.

South Korea has tried to engage the North

through tourism and the Gaeseong Industrial Complex project, but these projects have not lasted. In contrast, North Korea actively welcomes their Korean countrymen from all over the world. A special department within the government known as the Korean Expat Department is tasked with welcoming Korean Expats from other countries. Special guides are provided from the Korean Expat Department who speak the languages of the most populated countries that host Koreans from overseas. Koreans from China, Japan, Canada, the United States, Australia, and Russia are frequent visitors to North Korea. During major holidays, North Korea actively invites key members from these countries to attend their country's festivities with hotel accommodations and meals that are provided free of charge.

Discussions about unification are common among North Koreans. After our years in North Korea and having grown up in South Korea, it is clear to me that the two countries are quite fundamentally different. Their thinking, their culture, and even their language has diverged over the past seventy years. Politically, they are in stark contrast to each other with opposite economic systems and political ideologies.

One day I asked one of our North Korean

counterparts, "Would it be possible for North and South Korea to open their borders and co-exist as separate yet friendly nations?"

To my surprise, his reply was, "That is exactly what we are proposing! Our unification policy calls for separate yet equally respected countries. We are willing to allow two governments to exist. Since it is difficult for our two countries to agree upon the terms to be unified into a single nation, we are willing to co-exist in a friendly manner as two separate countries."

"Then, why isn't unification possible? That sounds like a good solution to me," I responded.

"South Korea will not accept these terms," he replied.

It's obvious that the issue of unification on the Korean Peninsula does not have a simple solution. North Korea is traumatized by the Korean War and South Korea by North Korea's militarism and human rights abuses. Neither country trusts the other.

North Korea is passionate about re-unification, but South Korea's policies towards North Korea change frequently. Passion for unification alone will probably not be enough to reunify the people of Korea. Both countries still refer to the other with their own names. South Korea refers to North

Korea as "Buk Han" or "North Han". Whereas, North Korea refers to South Korea as "Nam Chosun" or "South Chosun". If the two countries cannot even recognize each other's names, how are they going to cooperate in working through any of the deeper issues surrounding unification?

Regardless of whether or not there will ever be a political unification, it is evident that there is deep spiritual need for reconciliation. In order for there ever to be peace on the Korean Peninsula, both South and North Korea need to acknowledge each other's trauma and pain. When Korea finally faces her past, there will be hope for peace and reconciliation.

CHAPTER 15

North Korean Hearts and Minds

Our family lived and worked in North Korea for over ten years. Although we started in the Northeast Region of Rason, in 2013 we moved to the capital city of Pyongyang. We became the first American family to live in the Foreign Diplomatic Compound in Pyongyang and send our children to the Pyongyang Korean School for Foreigners. There were many firsts for our family, and I believe these milestones were only possible because of the trusting relationships we built with our North Korean colleagues.

I believe the humanitarian work we did in North Korea makes a difference. More importantly, I believe that it is the relationships we all build that will effect real change. The people of North Korea are genuinely interested in heart-felt relationships. It takes them a long time to trust a foreigner, but once they do, they are willing to move mountains for their friends.

Our family did not always live in the Foreign Diplomatic Compound. For the first four years in Pyongyang, we lived in an isolated, heavily guarded compound on the west side of the city. Our only neighbors were high-ranking military officials and the occasional foreign guest with whom we could not mingle. We had no freedom to leave the compound without the escort of our minders. It was a bleakly isolating existence. There was no grocery store, clinic, or other English-speaking neighbors on our compound. Our children had no friends to play with, and in the event of an emergency, we were at the mercy of our minder's availability and schedule.

After four years of what felt like house-arrest, we could no longer endure it. Work and home were all that we had for four years. We began to plead with our North Korean counterparts to be allowed to move to the Foreign Diplomatic Compound where we could at least have access to a grocery store and other foreigners. As U.S. citizens, with no formal diplomatic status in North Korea, we had no official standing to make such a request but we made it nonetheless.

One day, in the middle of these negotiations while Stephen was out of town for business, our minder showed up to our home with our driver. Thinking of the progress of our current negotiations, I invited them to stay for dinner and after the meal was done and the kids had gone off to play, the three of us sat around the dinner table a while. By this time, we had all been working together for about three years and were fairly comfortable with each other's company. The topic of the night drifted towards unification. As usual, I found myself in the middle of two cultures trying to explain to one side what they didn't understand about the other.

On this night as we discussed the possibility of unification between North and South Korea, I found myself explaining to my North Korean dinner guests why the idea of unification was so difficult for South Koreans to accept. I explained, "Just as you were traumatized by the Korean War, South Korea was too. For you, the enemy was the United States, but for South Korea the enemy was you. Before unification can take place, we all need to be able to forgive one another for the atrocities that occurred! If I could, I would ask forgiveness of you as a U.S. citizen, although I have no authority to do so. Please know that that is my heart. Only as we learn to forgive one another will unification be possible."

Our driver immediately agreed, "Definitely! If the U.S. can ask for forgiveness, then unification will surely be imminent!"

To my shock and dismay our minder then

added, "But of course, we have nothing we need to ask forgiveness for! Why should we ask for forgiveness?"

Although the conversation continued a while longer, it was obvious that I was hitting a wall when it came to their side of things. Out of frustration, silent tears started streaming down my face. At that point, our minder displayed obvious discomfort and quickly excused himself for the night.

On his way, he quietly asked me to walk him out. In the dark just outside our doorway and away from anyone else's ears, he did something I would have never expected in a million years. He apologized quietly and asked me not to cry. "I am sorry if I offended you. Please cheer up."

"It's not you," I replied. "I'm just frustrated. You are not the reason I am crying."

Impulsively he reached over and hugged me, repeating his apology. "Take heart! Cheer up! Please don't cry." Walls began to break down. Crossing all cultural lines, this North Korean man was hugging a white American woman, his enemy, reaching out in friendship.

A little later, we got unofficial word that we had an approximately one percent chance of moving to the Foreign Diplomatic Compound. It just would not be possible because of who we were.

This was confirmed by an official notice shortly afterwards. The final decision had been made. Our application to move to the Foreign Compound was denied. As I heard the news, I had to fight back the tears. However, Stephen and I had talked about this eventuality already. Together we'd decided what we would do if this was the result and so we calmly informed our minder that we would be leaving to take a break. Four years of isolation had taken its toll, and we could not carry on living like this.

To our utter amazement, two or three days later, before we'd even had a chance to start packing, our minder returned to tell us to pack our belongings. We were moving to the Foreign Compound! Bewildered, we did what we were told. Later we were officially told by our minder's superior what had changed the course of our housing decision.

When the news had come down that permission for us to move was denied, our minder had felt horrible. He knew how much we had sacrificed to live in Pyongyang, and more importantly he understood our hearts and trusted us. As a result, he immediately began writing a long letter of petition to appeal the decision. What was the content of his letter? It was about an American woman and her family and their sacrifice and heart for North Korea. His letter moved all of the officials involved in the decision process so deeply that they reversed their initial decision and granted our application all within just a few days! That was how our family ended up moving to the Foreign Diplomatic Compound as the first Americans to have lived there in almost seventy years!

The way we approach North Korea makes a difference. North Koreans are not interested in material help if accepting assistance means shaming their country and their people. North Koreans are a proud people, as are we all. Meaningful engagement with North Korea requires investment in trustworthy relationships.

How do we build trustworthy relationships with North Koreans? Simply by trying to understand where they come from and who they are. North Korea is not interested in being pitied or patronized by foreigners. They do not want to be told what to do. They want relationship based on mutual respect and reciprocal give and take.

Many North Koreans have been surprised to get to know us and interact with us. Their attitudes about Americans have changed from fear and hatred to openness and warmth for their newfound friends. The more my husband and I understood North Koreans, the more we learned to work together with positive results. And the more we learned to trust them, the deeper our relationships with them became.

To my own surprise, I discovered joy in building relationships in the DPRK. What became a personal journey of discovery has taught me so much about who I am. I had my own preconceptions of who North Koreans were, and not all of it was true. But I had preconceptions about myself too. It was only when I became vulnerable and allowed myself to engage openly with them on a human level in their own world that I began to expand my understanding of both North Koreans and of myself. Our journey into North Korea led to a paradigm shift in both of our hearts and minds. A collision of East and West brought about a brand-new worldview, and I find myself today full of gratitude in who I became during my ten years in North Korea.

ENDNOTES

1 Meyjes, Toby. "What would happen if war broke out between North Korea and the US?" *Metro*. April 11, 2017, accessed January 9, 2018.

2 Haltiwanger, John. "How Many People Would Die If Trump Went to War with North Korea?" *Newsweek*. September 27, 2017, accessed January 9, 2018.

3 Originally known as the Rajin-Sonbong Special Economic Zone in northeastern North Korea, the region was established in 1992 as open to international economic exchange. In 2000 the name was shortened to Rason. "Rason Special Economic Zone" Wikipedia. Accessed Sept 21, 2018 at https://en.wikipedia.org/wiki/Rason_Special_Economic_Zone. In 2013 and 2014 several smaller special economic zones were added throughout the country. Benjamin Katzeff Silberstein, Patrick M. Cronin (16 July 2018). "How the North Korean Economy Should - and Shouldn't - be Used in Negotiations". 38 North. The Henry L. Stimson Center. Accessed October 5 2018. https://www.38north.org/2018/07/bksilbersteinpcronin071618/.

4 Air Koryo is the official flagship airline of North Korea.

5 "The Grand Mass Gymnastics and Artistic Performance Arirang, also known as the Arirang Mass Games, or the Arirang Festival is a mass gymnastics and artistic festival held in the Rungrado May Day Stadium in Pyongyang, North Korea." From Wikipedia "Arirang Festival". Accessed Aug 10, 2018 at https://en.wikipedia.org/wiki/Arirang_Festival.

6 Wikipedia. "Altaic Languages", Accessed January 10, 2018. https://en.wikipedia.org/wiki/Altaic_languages.

7 Jin, Han-Jun, Tyler-Smith, Chris, and Wook Kim. The Peopling of Korea Revealed by Analyses of Mitochondrial DNA and Y-Chromosomal Markers. Plos One. January 16, 2009.

8 Wu, Mingren. "The Legendary Founder of Korea, Dangun Wanggeom." Ancient Origins Reconstructing the Story of Humanity's Past. February 17, 2016.

9 O'Connor, Tom. January 9, 2018. "NORTH KOREA SAYS NUCLEAR WEAPONS ONLY TARGET U.S., NOT RUSSIA, CHINA OR SOUTH KOREA AS TALKS BEGIN." *Newsweek*. Accessed October 5, 2018 at https://www.newsweek.com/north-korea-nuclear-weapons-only-target-us-not-russia-china-south-talks-775589.

10 Ibid.

11 Wikipedia. "Military History of Korea", Accessed January 10, 2018. https://en.wikipedia.org/wiki/Military_history_of_Korea.

12 Lankov, Andrei. War of Details. Korea Times. August 31, 2006, Accessed January 10, 2018. https://thegrandnarrative.com/2007/10/30/koreas-convenient-invasion-myths/.

13 Ibid.

14 Wikipedia. "Joseon", Accessed January 11, 2018. https://en.wikipedia.org/wiki/Joseon.

15 Ibid., note 14. Since the last dynasty of Korea was the Joseon Dynasty, North Korea kept the original name with different spelling in English as "Chosun". In English, the DPRK is Democratic People's Republic of Korea, but translated literally from Korean it is Chosun Democratic People's Republic.

16 The Three Kingdom Era of Korea consisted of Goguyreo, Shilla, and Baekje Dynasties (37 B.C.-918 A.D.). The southern part of Korea was divided between the Shilla and Baekje Dynasties, whereas the Goguryeo Dynasty was in the north. Koryeo, otherwise known as Goryeo, Dynasty (918 A.D.-1392 A.D.) governed the entire Korean Peninsula as well as parts of China. From Wikipedia "History of Korea". Accessed January 8, 2018. https://en.wikipedia.org/wiki/History_of_Korea.

17 Lee, Inyeop. "The War That Never Ended." *Soujourners*. September-October 2018. Accessed October 5, 2018. https://sojo.net/magazine/septemberoctober-2018/north-korea-war-never-ended-nuclear.

18 Ibid.

19 Talmadge, Eric. "64 Years After Korean War, North Still Digging Up Bombs." The Associated Press. July 25, 2017. Accessed October 5, 2018. https://www.semissourian.com/story/2430447.html.

20 Ibid.

21 Ibid.

22 Ibid.

23 Ibid.

24 Ibid.

25 Stack, Liam. Korean War, a 'Forgotten' Conflict That Shaped the Modern World. *New York Times*. January 1, 2018. Accessed October 5, 2018. https://www.nytimes.com/2018/01/01/world/asia/korean-war-history.html.

26 Wikipedia. "North Korea in the Korean War", Accessed January 12, 2018. https://en.wikipedia.org/wiki/North Korea_in_the_Korean_War.

27 Wikipedia. "North Korea Relations", Accessed January 15, 2018. https://en.wikipedia.org/wiki/Israel%E2%80%93North_Ko-rea_relations.

28 Wikipedia. "Rason Special Economic Zone", Accessed January 16, 2018. https://en.wikipedia.org/wiki/Rason_Special_Eco-nomic_Zone.

29 Lankov, Andrei. How North Koreans get rich on overseas labor jobs. NK *News*. January 16, 2018. Accessed October 5, 2018. https://www.nknews.org/2018/01/how-north-koreans-get-rich-on-overseas-labor-jobs/.

30 Wikipedia. "International Friendship Exhibition", Accessed January 16, 2018. https://en.wikipedia.org/wiki/International_Friendship_Exhibition.

31 "The festival was held annually between 2002 and 2013, with the exception of 2006. The mass games were not held in 2014, 2015, 2016, and 2017. Uri Tours announced in July 2018 that the mass games will return after a five-year hiatus, taking place from 9 September through 30 September. The title for 2018 is 빛나는 조국 ("The Glorious Country")." Wikipedia. Accessed September 4, 2018. https://en.wikipedia.org/wiki/Arirang_Festival.

32 Wikipedia. "Juche", Accessed January 19, 2018. https://en.wikipedia.org/wiki/Juche.

33 Ibid.

34 Wikipedia. "Nampo Dam", Accessed January 22, 2018. https://en.wikipedia.org/wiki/Nampo_Dam.

35 "...following DPRK leader Kim Jong Il's instruction in March 2003, which allowed for the transformation of farmers' markets into consolidated markets, the Unification Market opened as the largest market in Pyongyang on September 1st of the same year. With 1,500 booths spanning over 6000 sq. meters, the market is divided into three zones – agriculture produce and fish products, food and clothing, and metal utensils and appliances – with each zone housing a management office, money changer, and a food court, which offer a variety of conveniences to the customer." Pyongyang's 'Unification' Market of Today. NAPSNet Special Report. The Nautilus Institute for Security and Sustainability. Accessed September 13, 2018. https://nautilus.org/napsnet/napsnet-special-reports/pyongyangs-unification-market-of-today/.

36 "The Koryo Hotel is the top-ranked and second largest operating hotel in North Korea, the largest being the Yanggakdo Hotel." Wikipedia. Accessed September 13, 2018. https://en.wikipedia.org/wiki/Koryo_Hotel.

37 "North Korea ranks zero or near zero on all the usual freedom indices: freedom of public speech, private speech, public religious worship (the few churches are facades put up by the regime; the congregations consist of party spies and a few elderly people) ..." Kongdan Oh. "North Korea: The Nadir of Freedom" Foreign Policy Research Institute. May 10, 2007. Accessed September 13, 2018. https://www.fpri.org/article/2007/05/north-korea-the-nadir-of-freedom/.

38 "Organized religion is seen as a potential threat to the regime and therefore nothing apart from token churches built as a facade of religious freedom for foreign visitors are allowed." "The People's Challenges" North Korea 101. Liberty in North Korea. Accessed September 13, 2018. https://www.libertyinnorthkorea.org/learn-nk-challenges/.

39 Wikipedia. "Arch of Reunification", Accessed January 23, 2018. https://en.wikipedia.org/wiki/Arch_of_Reunification.

40 Wikipedia. "Gwangju Uprising", Accessed January 24, 2018. https://en.wikipedia.org/wiki/Gwangju_Uprising.

41 Kujath, Peter. South Korea cracks down on Kim sympathizers. Top Stories: *Asia*. July 13, 2012. Accessed October 5, 2018.

https://www.dw.com/en/south-korea-cracks-down-on-kim-sympathizers/a-16095785.

42 This is an anecdotal observation based on the personal account of the author's husband Stephen Yoon, recalling his memories of textbooks used during his childhood education in South Korea.

43 Wikipedia. "Ministry of Unification", Accessed January 25, 2018. https://en.wikipedia.org/Ministry_of_Unification.

PHOTOS

Chapter 1: Stephen and I in front of the Juche tower.

Chapter 2: Stephen and I on tarmac next to Air Koryo plane.

Chapter 3: Yong-Tong Sah, Buddhist Temple. Kaesong.

Chapter 4: Pal-Gol District. Pyongyang.

Chapter 5: Kim Il-sung Square. Pyongyang.

Chapter 6: The Juche Tower. Pyongyang.

Chapter 7: Harbor wall. Wonsan. DPRK.

Chapter 8: Sunset over Pyongyang.

Chapter 9: Mangyoungdae Amusement Park. Pyongyang.

Chapter 10: Bongsu Protestant Church. Pyongyang.

Chapter 11: Pyongyang Medical School Hospital, Pediatric Ward.

Chapter 12: Sports Day. Pyongyang Korean School for Foreigners.

Chapter 13: Mausoleum of Dangun. Kangdong.

Chapter 14: Three-Point Charter for National Reunification.

Chapter 15: Cherry Blossoms. Diplomatic Compound, Pyongyang.

Pyongyang Medical School Hospital. / Official meeting at Haebangsan Hotel.

Teaching children with disabilities.

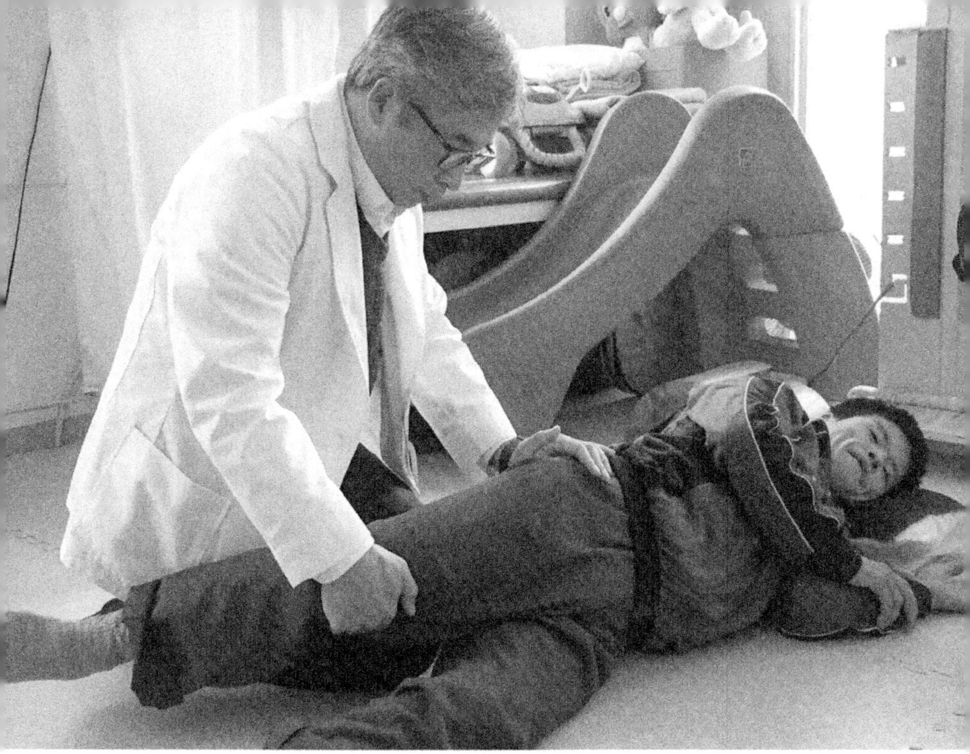

Treating patients with cerebral palsy.

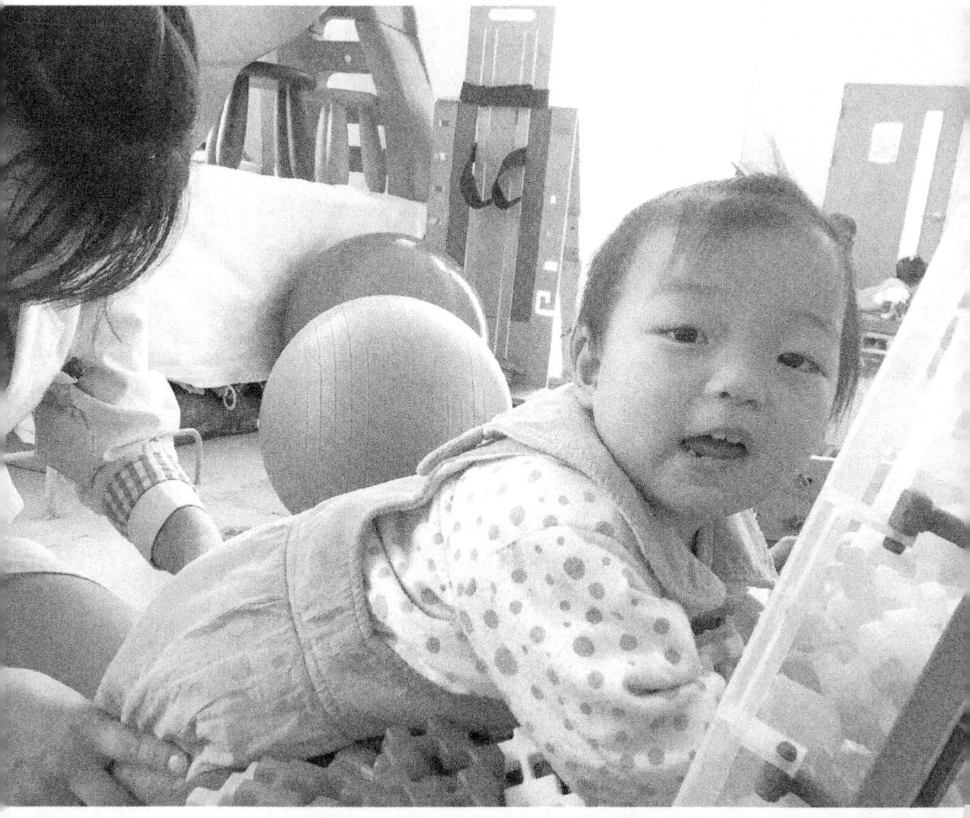

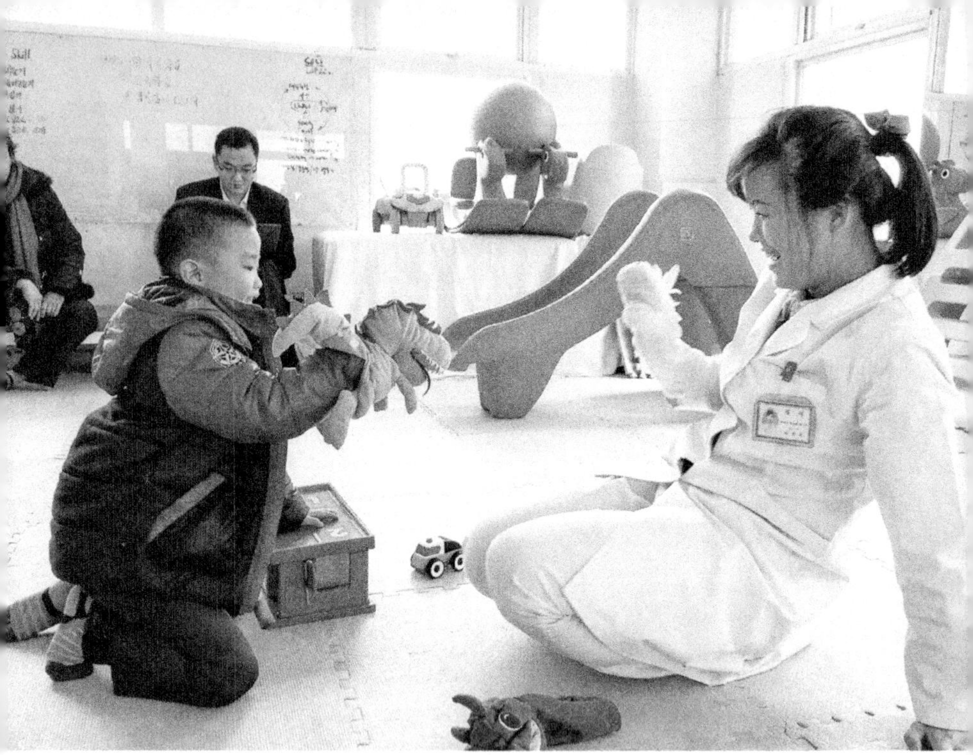

Encouraging social interaction from children with autism.

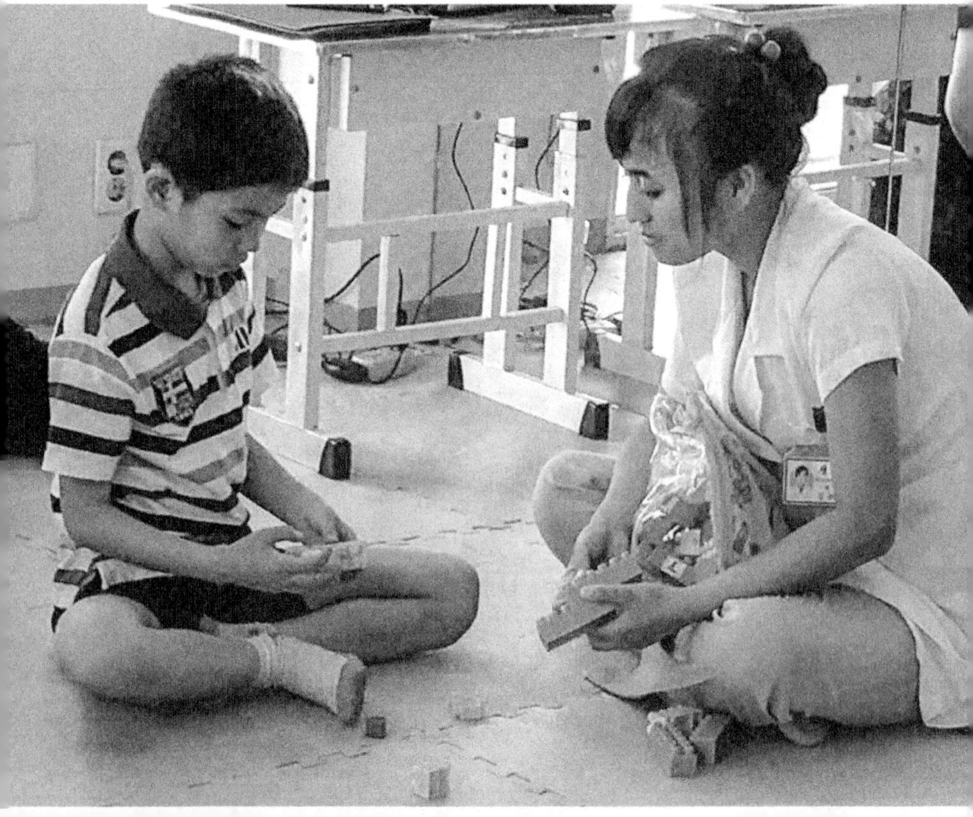

Teaching English as a second language.

Delivering and demonstrating rehabilitation equipment.

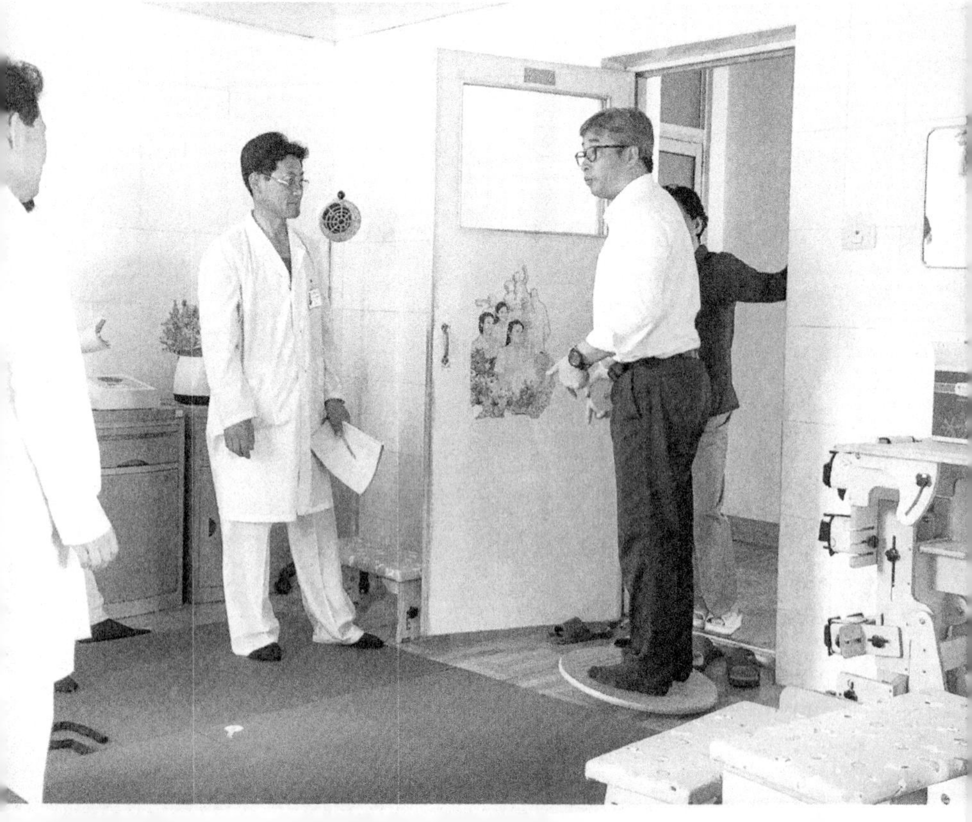

Teaching and training at Pyongyang Medical School Hospital.

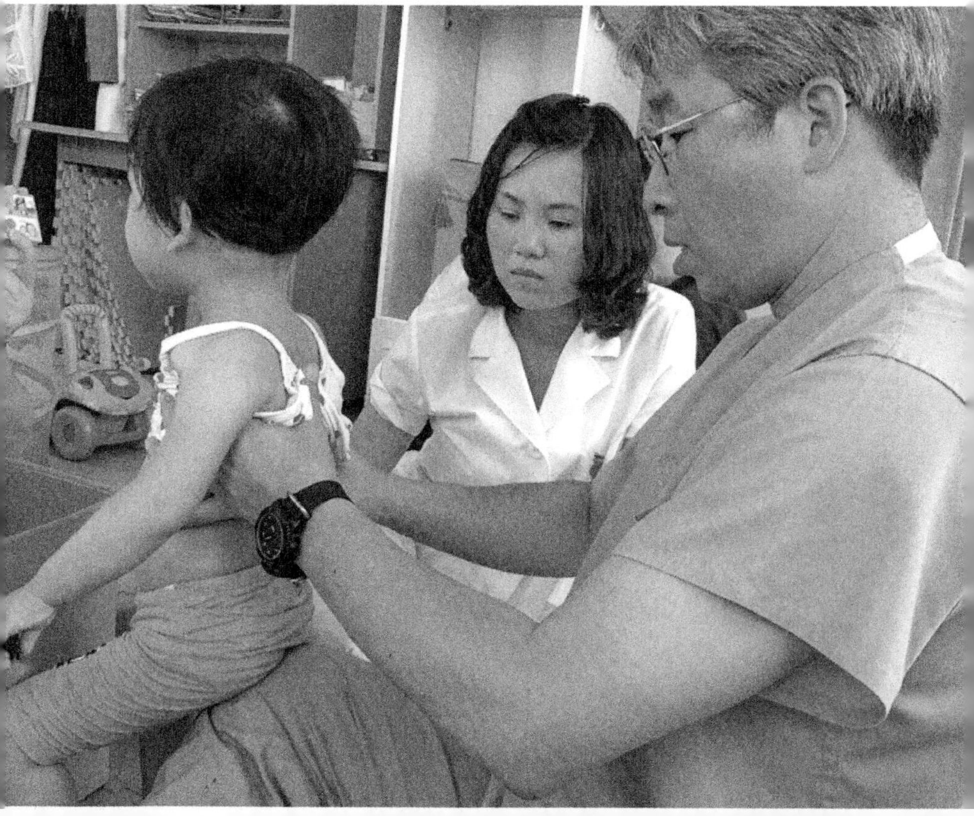